he Most Enabling Environment

Education Is for All Children

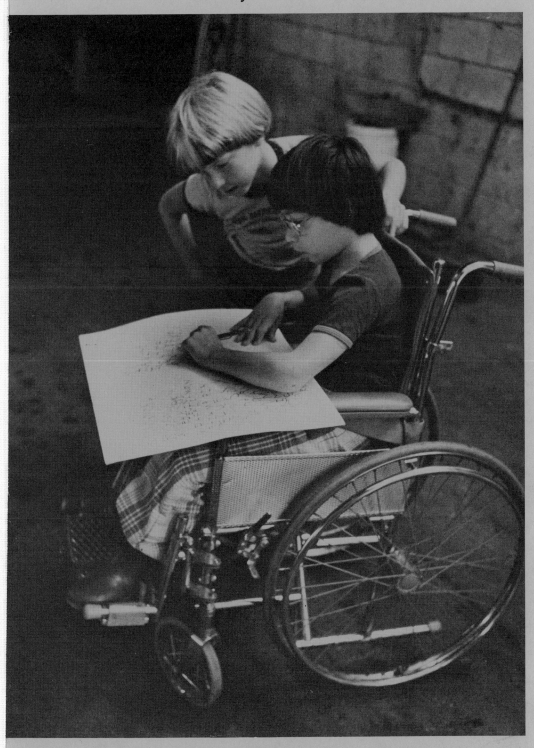

Association for Childhood Education International/$4.00

The Most Enabling Environment

Education Is for All Children

Editor: Sylvia Sunderlin
Acting Director of Publications: Lucy Prete Martin

Association for Childhood Education International
3615 Wisconsin Avenue, N.W., Washington, D.C. 20016

Acknowledgments

Subcommittee of the ACEI Publications Committee
responsible for initial planning of this bulletin:

Betty H. Waters, *Chairman*
Elementary Coordinator, Special Education, North Georgia College, Dahlonega

Harriet K. Cuffaro
Graduate Faculty, Bank Street College of Education, New York City

Tom Sills
Dean, School of Education, West Georgia College, Carrollton

Margaret G. Weiser
Associate Professor, Early Childhood Education, University of Iowa, Iowa City

Photographs:
Juliana Montfort
(cover, pp. 7, 16, 17, bottom of 23, 30, 33, 36, 38, 58, 62)

Nanda Ward Haynes, Director of Public Relations/Audiovisual Production
The Council for Exceptional Children, Reston, Virginia 22091
(pp. 5, top of 23, both on 44, 54)

*Special thanks are due these two photographers for their positive approach to viewing
children with handicaps in interaction with teachers, parents, and peers.*

Editor's Note: Although every reasonable care has been taken in this bulletin to
avoid the so-called "sexist" terminology, it has not always been possible to use
he/she or *his/hers* in speaking of the child. The editor has here and there used
the pronoun *he* to indicate the generic pronoun to mean a child of either sex,
rather than to interrupt the flow of prose with *he/she* or *him/her*.

Designer:
Susan Foster

Contents

Foreword

In 1958 our Association published *All Children Have Gifts*, a bulletin reflecting the agitation in education resulting from the launching of Sputnik by the Russians and the subsequent increased attention being placed on the education of the gifted. The publication emphasized the fact that *all children* have undiscovered potentialities and that democracy's assignment is to help them discover and develop their unique gifts.

Now, twenty years later, we find ourselves moving through another period of uncertainty and confusion as we try to provide appropriate educational programs for the handicapped, a group of children within our society that has been neglected by our public institutions. Again the ACEI Publications Committee has responded to the needs of our members by developing a bulletin speaking directly to questions related to the implementation of Public Law 94-142, the Education for All Handicapped Children Act of 1975.

The authors of this new publication explore in depth the immediate implications of P.L. 94-142 for the children, parents and teachers who will be most affected by its provisions. They also help us examine the legislation from a more comprehensive point of view and conclude that "the most enabling environment" must be our goal for all children. The Association greatly appreciates the contribution each author has made to the bulletin.

Many persons have been involved in the development of *The Most Enabling Environment: Education Is for All Children* through discussion at ACEI conferences and at meetings held at our Washington, D.C., headquarters. The group most actively involved in its final stages, however, was a subcommittee of the Publications Committee composed of Betty Waters, Elementary Coordinator, Special Education, North Georgia College, Dahlonega; Margaret G. Weiser, Associate Professor, Early Childhood Education, University of Iowa, Iowa City; Harriet K. Cuffaro, Graduate Faculty, Bank Street College of Education, New York City; and Tom Sills, Dean, School of Education, West Georgia College, Carrollton.

Special thanks go to Vito Perrone, Dean, Center for Teaching and Learning, University of North Dakota, Grand Forks, who served as a consultant to the subcommittee; to Dorothy H. Cohen, Senior Faculty, Graduate Programs, Bank Street College of Education, New York City, who gave assistance in the final planning; and to Sylvia Sunderlin, editor extraordinary, who worked from the subcommittee's outline in coordinating the development of this publication.

A word of appreciation also to Monroe D. Cohen, former Director of Publications/Editor, whose constant concern for all children is reflected in the title and theme of this bulletin.

ROBERT GILSTRAP
Professor of Education
George Mason University, Fairfax, Virginia
and
Chairman, Publications Committee

Introduction

Freeing Every Child's Potential

ELIZABETH H. BRADY
Professor, Department of Educational Psychology
California State University, Northridge

The initial reaction to passage of the Education for All Handicapped Children Act of 1975 was triumph. In the early days after its passage, citizens, legislators and parents, who had fought long and hard to achieve such legislation (Kirk 1978), expressed unqualified enthusiasm. At last one of our largest minorities was to be provided for.

During the sobering observations of four intervening years, many have raised voices in response to the Act. Some have continued euphoric praise; others have made dire predictions. Many have addressed the concerns of special interest groups, not the handicapped themselves as much as their parents who out of ignorance may be deprived of their rights; or their teachers, who may feel unqualified and anxious over new demands for performance (Ashley 1977); or their nonhandicapped classmates, who may be deprived of financial resources and teacher attention once handicapped children begin to be served. Still others have focused on legal issues, allocations of responsibility, and funds.

Some of the polemics and forecasts of doom clearly arise from misinformation or misinterpretation of the provisions of the Act. Other comments represent honest assessment of the difficulties of implementation, weighed against a background of experience with education and legislation. In any event, it is now clear to all thoughtful persons that P.L. 94-142 is a complex law and that its implementation will be slow and will involve issues and decisions not initially foreseen.

Our intention in this bulletin is to clarify what the Act is, whom it affects, how it can be interpreted, its goals and aims and implications for teachers and parents as well as children. We wish also to identify issues and problems that should be anticipated.

The language of the Act (P.L. 94-142) calls for providing each handicapped child with the "least restrictive environment" for learning. Some have been quick to interpret this phrase as meaning that all handicapped children will be "mainstreamed" into regular classrooms. The term "mainstreaming" itself is being widely used to stand for the entire Act, without regard to the alternatives that should be considered in careful implementation. In this interpretation, freeing every child's potential means freedom *from* separation from nonhandicapped, *from* special programs, *from* any plan that provides for other than regular classroom placement.

6

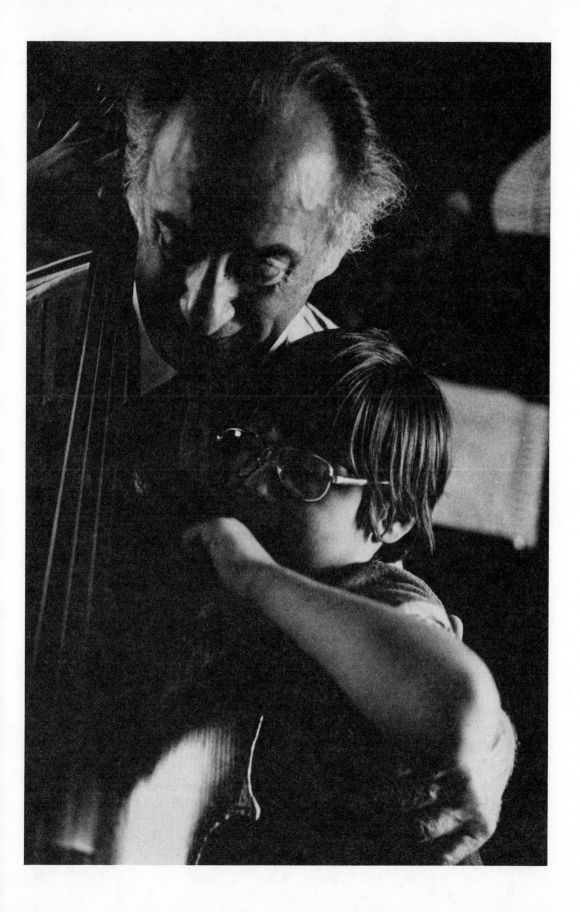

Such interpretation could lead to unfortunate distortion of the intent of the law. Not every child will learn and grow best when mainstreamed into a regular classroom. The intent of the law is that each child will be planned for according to what will be best for him and, by extension, best for those persons affected by what is planned and carried out for him.

The title of this bulletin, *The Most Enabling Environment: Education Is for All Children,* conveys a more positive tone than does the term "least restrictive environment." It also reflects an alternative conception of what freedom is, a concept articulated by John Dewey in *Freedom and Conduct* (1929), who pointed out that freedom, far from being some idealized state of affairs untainted by rules and restrictions, means "freedom in and among actual events, not apart from them." Further, "the road to freedom may be found in that knowledge of facts which allows us to employ them in connection with desires and aims." He concluded his essay: "We use the foresight of the future to refine and expand present activities. In this use of desire, deliberation and choice, freedom is actualized."

It is with this concept of freedom that we approach the discussion of the education of handicapped children. We are concerned with what must be understood and what ought to be foreseen, with what realities must be taken into account and what problems and pitfalls can be anticipated so that choices can be made in realizing the aims of development and learning for all children.

Variations from State to State

Although P.L. 94-142 is federal legislation, implementation will differ from place to place, as states continue to have direct control over educational policy. States differ enormously with respect to existing laws and educational plans affecting the handicapped (such as the Master Plan for Special Education in California), in financial resources, qualified teachers and supervisors and facilities for teacher education, community attitudes and experience, the existence of alternative educational resources, public or private. There may exist regulations or policies inconsistent with the intent of the law, such as an organizational structure for funding and administration, which in effect violates the requirement not to label children in terms of handicaps. These will have to be analyzed and possibly altered.

Rights of Children and Parents

Many regard the law as primarily a civil rights act. There are excellent provisions for nondiscriminatory procedures in assessment, for due process and fair hearings, which parents may use on behalf of their child. Yet emphasis on these aspects of the Act without acknowledgment of fiscal and procedural realities could result in delay and even reduction of appropriate program implementation for children.

Ideally, parents and school systems will be partners in providing the most enabling environment for each child. Both can and should be advocates on his behalf. But the realities of limited funding, unprepared teachers and lack of organization may initially create circumstances in which it will appear to parents that the school is unwilling to serve their child. If this threat occurs and the parents and the schools are forced into adversary positions, everyone will lose.

The Individualized Education Program

At the heart of the implementation is the individualized education program (IEP). Such a program is to be prepared for each child on the basis of careful assessment of the child and shall constitute a program to be followed, not mere guidelines. A classroom teacher must be involved in the planning, not necessarily the child's own teacher. It is not surprising that many teachers are apprehensive about what this will mean to them personally. It is important that they understand that teacher accountability has been separated from the question of how successfully the plan works and how well the child learns.

Even though the law does not require it, it is important that the teacher who will work with the child be part of the process of assessment and planning. Unfortunately in this complex world of guidelines, legal specifications and concerns for accountability, there is too much reliance on simply complying, even when knowledge of the needs of persons involved would suggest we do more and better than the law requires. The sensitivity of administrators to such teacher-child relationships will powerfully influence implementation.

No matter how carefully the IEP is prepared, not every situation can be fully anticipated. We cannot predict the perfect mix in mainstreaming, for example, either for the child with the handicap or for others in the group. Some characteristics that deeply affect interpersonal relations are not readily identified or quantified. Feelings and fears can be unexpectedly triggered. It is fundamental from the beginning of implementing IEP to realize that it may be necessary to reassess, to make changes in plans and to keep program development open-ended.

All Children Can Benefit

One way in which implementation can serve *all* children is that it can force re-examination of existing practices currently taken for granted. In an article in *American Education* (1976) a query was raised as to whether an IEP would soon be required for *every* child, handicapped or not. Is this not, in fact, what ought to happen? We have talked a great deal in recent years about *individualizing* and *personalizing*. Too often this has been mere lip service, corrupted in the service of a management system or sequenced materials in which only the pace of learning was varied, not the content or the learning mode or the personal style of the learner. True attention to individual differences is a continuing and growing need in education in increasingly complex and stressful settings. (Gordon 1978)

The ACEI philosophy expounded in the 1958 bulletin *All Children Have Gifts* that individualizing and personalizing education are necessary to free every child's potential is poignantly applicable in 1979. The "creativeness. . .present in some degree in every child" is just as true of the child with a handicap as it is of the nonhandicapped child.

When teachers discover that careful observation, planning for the need of each child based upon child study, and organizing instruction to facilitate teaching to individual needs all meet with approval, we will be on our way to more meaningful education for every child. This is a long-range goal requiring more human and material resources than we now allocate to education.

Realistic Regard for the Handicapped

American Education (Hoyt 1978) carried an enthusiastic article about the film series *Feeling Free*, designed to help children understand handicaps and to explore assumptions many persons, including the handicapped, hold about others who are handicapped. Five children with differing handicaps were selected for their appeal as actors or because they had qualities of making others want to know them. One can understand these criteria in designing effective mass media presentations, but there may be a danger in overemphasizing the charm or attractiveness of the handicapped. In reality, not all handicapped children are beguiling, any more than are all nonhandicapped children. Certain anomolies or injuries result in physically unattractive conditions that may elicit reactions of fear or revulsion from others, both children and adults.

Too often we proffer acceptance or approval if a person has some redeeming virtue or characteristic despite his being slow, clumsy, or in other ways is unable to match qualities valued by his peers. Welcoming the handicapped child because he is in some way special in a positive sense may be a kind of artificial, conditional acceptance. Each of us hopes for and deserves better.

Sometimes fear and dislike of a person who is different are manifest in our attributing to him feelings that are "just like everybody else's." But handicapped persons often do not feel like everybody else. They may have chronic anger, may feel they have been singled out to be miserable, avoided by others, dealt with unfairly. These are real feelings not always understood or even apparent to others who do not experience their frustrations.

Every child can benefit from the provisions of the Act. To the extent that the nonhandicapped child plays with, learns with, interacts with handicapped children in an educational setting, he will benefit by acquiring a broader view of humanity, a more sympathetic appreciation of what the handicapped can and cannot do.

I have had the opportunity to observe the evolution of DEAL (Dual Educational Approach to Learning) over the past eight years at the Salvin School in the Los Angeles Unified School District. In this program non-handicapped children starting at age three have been integrated into early childhood education programs with children who were orthopedically handicapped, mentally retarded, sometimes deaf or hearing impaired, or multiply handicapped. My observations convinced me that:

Nonhandicapped children benefit socially and emotionally from being with handicapped children in an educational setting.

Handicapped children experience rich and appropriate learning opportunities and social-emotional development when nonhandicapped children join them.

Both benefits were possible because this educational setting and program were developmentally sound for children, using both child-chosen and teacher-chosen learning activities.

Most of us suffer from too limited contacts with our fellow men. Our professional duties, social patterns, modes of transportation often isolate us from other races, poor people, the handicapped, the infirm, the old. Gradually this is changing, as it is in my own community, with new facilitating arrangements for the handicapped, with affirmative action and financial support programs. Although change is painfully gradual, our community is becoming more diverse.

For every child greater heterogeneity in his contacts with others is desirable so that he may struggle with the meaning of differences, not only between him and the girl in his class who is blind or the boy with a speech impediment. Children are always "trying to make sense" out of their world. The richer and more varied their experiences of others, the more chance they will have to puzzle through the complexities of human life.

For the nonhandicapped child the educational setting must provide adults who can listen, observe with him, answer questions and support his tentative explorations in understanding what other human beings are like.

And Teachers Benefit Too

"What a piece of work is a man!" observed Hamlet. In the sixties youth celebrated this truth in a moving song from the musical comedy *Hair*. Day by day it is easy to lose sight of how truly remarkable human beings are. As teachers we often take for granted the sometimes predictable learning and development of children. Opportunities to work with and teach handicapped children, observe the persistence and effort they bring to accomplishment of what we have come to think of as easy and natural, can reawaken us as teachers to appreciate what an extraordinary thing it is to be a human being.

11

References

Ashley, Joyce G. "Mainstreaming: One Step Forward, Two Steps Back." *American Educator,* Vol. 1, No. 3, October, 1977.

Dewey, John. "What Is Freedom?" *Human Nature and Conduct.* Modern Library Edition, 1929. Pp 303-309.

Gordon, Edmund W. "Toward a Conceptualization of Urban Education." *IRCD Bulletin,* Vol. XIII, No. 3, Summer, 1978. N.Y.: Teachers College, Columbia University.

Hoyt, Jane Hauser. "Feeling Free." *American Education.* Vol. 14, No. 9, November, 1978. United States Department of Health, Education and Welfare.

Kirk, Samuel A. "The Federal Role in Special Education: Historical Perspectives." Frank M. Hewett and Barbara K. Keogh (Eds.), *Rights of a Special Minority,* in *Educator,* Graduate School of Education, U.C.L.A. Vol. 20, No. 2, Spring/Summer, 1978.

I. *Bringing Them into the Mainstream*

Who Are the Handicapped?

BONNIE DOWNES LEONARD
Associate Professor, Graduate School of Education
Lesley College, Cambridge, Massachusetts

In America certain children are identified as handicapped by our legal code.

The term "handicapped children" means mentally retarded, hard of hearing, deaf, speech impaired, visually impaired, or health impaired children, or children with specific learning disabilities, who by reason thereof require special education and related services. (P.L. 94-142, Education for All Handicapped Children Act of 1975)

In a nonliterate society, children with "specific learning disabilities," who exhibit difficulties in reading, writing and spelling, would not be labeled as handicapped. Even in our own literate American culture, many children are not labeled or diagnosed as having specific learning disabilities until they are placed in an environment that demands literacy, that is, until they go to school. "Specific learning disabilities" falls in the mild-to-moderate range of handicapping conditions in our society, but even the most extreme disabling conditions might not be labeled "handicapped" in another culture. Over four decades ago Benedict (1934) commented on this important truism:

One of the most striking facts that emerge from a study of widely varying cultures is the ease with which our abnormals function in other cultures. It does not matter which kind of "abnormality" we choose for illustration, those which indicate extreme instability, or those which are more in the nature of character traits like sadism or delusions of grandeur or of persecution, there are well-described cultures in which these abnormals function at ease and with honor, and apparently without danger or difficulty to society.—R. Benedict, "Anthropology and the Abnormal," *Journal of General Pscyhology, 10,* 1934, p. 63. By permission.

Labeling and Diagnosis

In our society, the classification of handicapped children bears the imprimatur of medical science. Labeling of exceptionality has either been the prerogative of the medical profession or has reflected its orientation toward pathology and disease. Phenomena that in other times might have been called the work of the devil are now considered sicknesses. Handicapped children are "diagnosed" and "treated," and "prescriptions" are written for them with comments on "prognosis" and "etiology." The assumptions implicit in this medical perspective are the same whether a child is said to be blind or moderately retarded. This clinical view holds that the handicapping condition or disease lies within the person and that knowledge of the etiology of the disease leads to a specific treatment plan. (Mercer 1973)

The medical model is probably most workable when the handicapping condition has a known and simple etiology. Rutter (1978) distinguished three types of handicapping conditions on the basis of etiology. The first is a "single condition" such as Down's syndrome or phenylketonuria (PKU). The etiology of these conditions is known and in the case of phenylketonuria, early diagnosis and intervention (a carefully controlled diet) can eliminate an ensuing retardation. While amniocentesis can provide information about the chromosomal abnormality that signals Down's syndrome, there is no cure at present, and the question of whether or not to abort the fetus is ethical rather than medical. The treatment of children with Down's syndrome has no clear specification, since such individual factors as variance of IQ (there are Down's syndrome children with IQ's in the average range) profoundly affect any treatment decisions.

The second type of disorder Rutter (1978) defines is "a behavioral syndrome without a single cause, but nevertheless with a common biological causation." Such is the case with cerebral palsy, a term generally used to mean any abnormality of motor functioning that is the result of brain defect, injury or disease. Plans for treating children with cerebral palsy include the traditional approaches of occupational and physical therapy, as well as the more controversial techniques of Dolman and Delcato at the Institute for Human Potential in Philadelphia. Parents of children with cerebral palsy, seeking professional help for their children, are often bewildered by a lack of a common or direct approach to their children's therapy.

The third type of disorder outlined by Rutter (1978) is "the end product of a wide and heterogeneous range of factors, both biological and psychosocial," pointing to language delay and reading difficulties as examples, since they may be the result of "brain damage, genetic influence, or lack of stimulation." Treatment for these last examples of handicap is extremely varied and belongs under the aegis of educators rather than physicians, since etiology is vague, diffuse, and only tenuously related to treatment. Determining whether the cause of a child's reading disorder is developmental delay, minimal brain dysfunction, psychogenic, or a combination of factors is far more speculative in prescribing treatment than in the case of prescribing the diet for phenylketonuria.

The limitations of the medical model are most apparent to teachers and parents who have the daily task of living and working with handicapped children. As one parent of an "autistic" child so aptly comments:

Perhaps this would not be true if the professionals had access to a sure body of knowledge about psychotic or defective children, which they could have imparted to us. But they did not, nor did they pretend to. What they had was a body of observations, some of it crystallized into theory, on the behavior of a large number of children and what appeared to affect it. These children were different from Elly and from each other; conclusions drawn from their problems or solutions were of doubtful applicability to this particular child.—C.C. Park, *The Seige,* Harcourt Brace. 1967. By permission of Colin Smythe Ltd., Gerrards Cross, Bucks, England.

For well over a decade some social scientists (Freidson 1970, Mechanic 1968 and Szasz 1964) have been questioning the validity of the medical model. The social systems perspective these social scientists propose accentuates the *culture-bound nature* of mental and, perhaps, even physical disorders. (Scheff 1975)

From the basis of the social systems theory, new definitions of handicap evolve with the changing mores of society. During the sixties, a decade of marked social change in America, the labels of deviance, including mental and physical disorders, underwent revision. In 1961, the American Association on Mental Deficiency (AAMD) Manual on Terminology and Classification in Mental Retardation defined mental retardation as "sub-average general functioning which originated during the developmental period and is associated with impairment in adaptive behavior." "Sub-average general functioning" was operationalized as a score greater than *one* standard deviation below the mean on a standardized test. In 1973, the AAMD Manual defined retardation as "subaverage general intellectual functioning existing concurrently with deficits in adaptive behavior, and manifested during the developmental period." "Subaverage general functioning" was now determined by a cut-off point of *two* standard deviations below the mean (Filler, Robinson, Smith, Vincent-Smith, Bricker & Bricker 1975). This fluctuation of standard deviation in deter-mining retardation was a barometer of the changing social attitudes.

The Socioculturally Handicapped

With the eyes of America focused on social injustice, it is not surprising that the identification of the handicapped should come under scrutiny. The possibility of prejudicial practice was raised. In 1968, Dunn estimated that sixty to eighty percent of the pupils enrolled in classes for the mildly retarded were from low status backgrounds, "including Afro-Americans, American Indians, Mexicans, and Puerto-Rican Americans, those from nonstandard English speaking, broken, disorganized and inadequate homes, and children from other nonmiddle-class environments." In an ambitious project designed to determine the prevalence of mental retarda-tion in Riverside, California, Mercer (1973) reported that children labeled

as retarded by the public schools had twice as many blacks and four-and-a-half times as many Mexican Americans than might be expected from their proportion in the general population. Obversely, only half as many Anglo children were labeled as retarded.

Johnson (1975) reviewed studies examining age, sex, and social class in relation to categories of mental retardation, emotional disturbance and learning disabilities. From her review, she hypothesized that "the younger child is more likely to be classified as learning disabled, while the older child is more likely to be considered retarded," that "a girl is more likely to be retarded than learning disabled," and that "lower class children are more likely to be considered retarded than learning disabled." She suggested that sociocultural factors are more likely to "sort children into categories when psychoeducational information is ambiguous."

Segments of Public Law 94-142 speak to past transgressions of sociocultural inequity by requiring that assessment of a child's handicap be racially and culturally nondiscriminatory and, where applicable (as in Hispanic-Americans), that testing be done in the primary language of the child. Parents are to be given a say in the evaluation and placement of their children as well as the right to protest placement decisions.

There are other discriminatory practices, however, in what might be called "secondary labeling." Once a child is described as "deaf" or "health impaired" or "orthopedically impaired" or any of the other labels of disability, he enters the realm of the handicapped. As a member of the handicapped minority in society, that child may be subject to all the attendant

Boy with protecting helmet works away from his wheelchair, using support board.

cruelties of discrimination, however subtle. How easy, for example, to equate physical slowness with mental retardation! With this kind of "secondary labeling," one negative trait implies another.

This "secondary labeling" is reinforced and even promulgated by the larger perspective of media. Television, America's most powerful mass medium, not only reflects cultural values, but also serves to maintain and even perpetuate them. In a study examining television portrayal of handicapped persons on prime-time dramatic shows, handicapped characters were distinguished from nonhandicapped characters by dimensions other than their physical and mental disabilities. (Leonard 1978). They were demographically seen as lower-class, unemployed, and single. As a group they were depicted personally as uncultured, stupid, impatient, and lacking in self-confidence; and they were portrayed physically as sloppy in dress, passive and weak. Their physical passivity was mirrored in their presentation as dependent and submissive in their interactions with other characters. Such distortions add brutal secondary characteristics to the primary ones of disability and can serve no purpose other than to fortify the barriers that separate handicapped from nonhandicapped in our society.

The boundaries that distinguish the handicapped vary with time and place. Persons marked as exceptional in one society may be ordinary or unremarkable in another. But in all societies the identification of "handicapped" persons is a political, economic and social phenomenon that is often prejudicial to those less powerful, less affluent and less integrated into the mainstream.

References

Benedict, R. "Anthropology and the Abnormal." *Journal of General Psychology*, 1934, *10*, 59-82.

Dunn, L.M. "Special Education for the Mildly Retarded—Is Much of It Justifiable?" L.D. Stoppleworth (Ed.), *Everything Is Fine Now That Leonard Isn't Here.* New York: MSS Information Co., 1973.

Freidson, E. *Professional Dominance.* Chicago: Aldine, 1970.

Filler, J.W., C.C. Robinson, R.A. Smith, L.J. Vincent-Smith, D. Bricker and W.A. Bricker. "Mental Retardation." N. Hobbs (Ed.), *Issues in the Classification of Children,* Vol. I. San Francisco: Jossey Bass, 1975.

Johnson, V. "Salient Features and Sorting Factors in Diagnosis and Classification of Exceptional Children." *Peabody Journal of Education,* 1975, 2, 142-149.

Leonard, B.D. "Impaired View: Television Portrayal of Handicapped People," (Doctoral dissertation, Boston University, 1978.) *Dissertation Abstracts International,* 1978, 39, No. 7819756.

Mechanic, D. *Medical Sociology: A Selective View.* New York: Free Press, 1968.

Mercer, J. *Labeling the Mentally Retarded.* Berkeley: University of California Press, 1973.

Park, C.C. *The Seige.* New York: Harcourt, Brace and World, 1967.

Rutter, M. "Diagnosis and Definition." M. Rutter and E. Schopler (Eds.), *Autism: A Reappraisal of Concepts and Treatment.* New York: Plenum Press, 1978.

Scheff, T.J. *Labeling Madness.* Englewood Cliffs, N.J.: Prentice-Hall, 1975.

Szasz, T. *The Myth of Mental Illness.* New York: Harper & Row, 1964.

Interpreting Public Law 94-142

MAYNARD C. REYNOLDS
Professor, Department of Psychoeducational Studies
University of Minnesota, Minneapolis

Public Law 94-142, the Education for All Handicapped Children Act of 1975, reflects the shift in public policy toward minority groups, which began with the Supreme Court decision in *Brown* v. *Board of Education* (1954) and proceeded through a series of issue-oriented adjudications (Gilhool 1976; Weintraub, Abeson, Ballard & LaVor 1976). The law essentially obligates the states, for the first time in the history of public education in the United States, to provide free and appropriate individualized education for all handicapped children and youth, regardless of severity of handicap; to educate such children with their nonhandicapped peers to the maximum extent possible; and to protect the procedural rights of handicapped children and their parents in all matters of school assessment and placement.

Sudden shifts in public policy are not easily implemented. A quarter of a century has elapsed since segregation in the schools was outlawed, yet racial balance is still an issue in many school districts across the country. When P.L. 94-142 was signed into law, the states were given a two-year grace period to prepare plans for the education of handicapped children; nevertheless, when the law became effective,[1] only a relatively small proportion of the schools were ready for full compliance. Among the obstacles to active compliance were taxpayers' protests against the rising cost of education despite decreasing enrollment, the lack of preparation among school personnel to assume new roles and follow new practices, and a general misunderstanding of the provisions of the law among both the public and educators. One popular misconception that arouses opposition is that P.L. 94-142 authorizes the wholesale "mainstreaming"of handicapped children in regular classrooms without adequate supports from special educators.

Aside from its sweeping mandate, P.L. 94-142 reflects the tremendous improvement within a generation in the skills and procedures for delivering special education. Starting in the 1960s, a number of far-seeing special

---

[1]Procedural requirements began in Fall, 1977; full obligations to serve all children in the age range 3-18 became effective Fall, 1978. Beginning in Fall, 1980, the upper age limit will be 21.

educators began experimenting with methods of providing services to children with various learning handicaps in regular classrooms, sometimes employing special learning centers or "resource rooms." (Deno 1972) These programs were of special significance because even at the best of times there were never enough special education teachers to serve all children with special learning needs in self-contained classes. Consequently, during the 1960s and early 1970s, a number of states and school districts adopted the principle of normalizing education for handicapped students to the fullest possible extent and de-emphasizing placements in special settings. Some practices perfected in these settings were incorporated into the mandates of P.L. 94-142.

Another distinct advance in special education over recent decades has been the widespread development of competently managed programs for severely handicapped children, a development so impressive that legislators found it reasonable to extend the concept of *right* to education literally to all students.

Basic Concepts of P.L. 94-142

The culmination of what Dimond (1973) characterized as a "quiet revolution" occurred when P.L. 94-142 established legislatively the principle that every handicapped child, regardless of the severity of the handicap, has the *right to education.* Previously, schools have had the privilege of refusing to admit children for whom no programs were provided or who were considered "unteachable." The corollary to this principle is the mandate in P.L. 94-142 to schools to *find, locate, and evaluate* every handicapped child in the age range 3-21.

The Act's emphasis that education should be *appropriate* to the individual implies that the purpose of education is the enhancement of the individual's life. Appropriate education is to be carried out by requiring that school personnel and parents write out an *Individualized Education Program* (IEP) for each handicapped child, and by providing special education and related services. Indeed, one of the stated purposes of the Act is "to assure that all handicapped children have available to them. . .a free appropriate public education which emphasizes special education and related services designed to meet their unique needs." (Sec. 3(c))

The law also requires the placement of handicapped children according to the principle of the *least restrictive alternative.* Each state plan is required to assure that "to the maximum extent appropriate," (Sec. 612(5)) handicapped children will be educated with their nonhandicapped peers and will be removed from this regular educational environment only if it is established that another environment is more promising for them.

Handicapped children and/or their parents or guardians must participate in all decisions affecting the children and in the writing of IEPs. The *due process* rights of the parents and children must be observed.

20

The states are required to establish priorities for providing educational services to handicapped children, first, to those who are not receiving education, and second, to those whose education is inadequate.

Testing and evaluation materials and procedures that are racially or culturally discriminatory are prohibited; testing must be carried out in the child's primary language; and no single test or procedure may be the sole criterion for determining a child's appropriate educational placement or program.

In recognition of the lack of preparation of most school personnel to fulfill the provisions of the Act, Sec. 513(3) mandates that the states provide comprehensive systems of personnel development, including inservice training.

State departments of education and local educational agencies that comply with P.L. 94-142 and submit approved plans for the education of handicapped children to the U.S. Office of Education receive federal funds on a per capita basis. Over the next several years, the amount of funds will be substantial but, as is often the case with federal programs, authorizations tend to outstrip appropriations. For fiscal year 1979 the federal appropriation for support of programs relating to P.L. 94-142 is $804 million.

Compliance

So far, the responses in the schools to the new policies and procedures have been uneven from one community to another. In some school districts teachers have been given "quickie" lessons in how to write IEPs and obtain parents' signatures of approval, actions geared to "staying out of jail" or minimal compliance with the law. Where compliance is least, the attitude seems to be that P.L. 94-142 is just another educational fad that will run its course and disappear. Those holding this point of view, however, appear to underestimate the force of the constitutional and other judicial interpretations upon which P.L. 94-142 is based.

In other school systems, full compliance is hampered by the lack of adequate support personnel and budget restrictions. Although many boards of education have hailed the law for permitting savings in school operations by trimming down the largely separate special education system, P.L. 94-142 may, in fact, turn out to be more costly. One reason is that even when handicapped children are served in the mainstream they usually need special education delivered in the regular classroom. More children with complex learning problems are being returned to the communities from residential and special schools, requiring reinforcements of special education and other services. Since blind children with no other handicaps are now placed only rarely in residential schools, appropriate educational services usually involving teachers of braille, mobility, and orientation, must be provided for them in community schools.

Returning orthopedically handicapped children to local buildings from special schools usually necessitates removal of architectural barriers and the adaptation of rest rooms. In other school districts, the increasing numbers of handicapped children who have not heretofore been provided with services or who have been inadequately served, are creating enormous funding difficulties.

Efforts at Compliance

In those places where active compliance with the law is under way, certain trends can be noted that hold promise for the future. Despite the great burden that implementation of the Act has imposed on many schools, great efforts are being made in many schools, in many states, to comply fully with the law. Special education cooperatives have been organized, for a good example of diligent resourcefulness, to bring services of specialists to rural and suburban schools where there is scarcity of such personnel.

There is also a movement to decentralize special education so that the services can be provided in many places rather than a few. School psychologists and other specialists are being detached from their clinics and classes and are moving into the schools to work closely with classroom teachers as well as children. One fruitful arrangement is the establishment of consulting relationships between classroom teachers and special educators. In these relationships, the special education teacher may work directly with handicapped children for part of the day in resource rooms, then spend the rest of the day consulting with teachers on classroom problems.

Regular classroom teachers are not always happy about giving up the autonomy of the self-contained classroom. Most teachers in the schools today were trained in the techniques of managing alone the education of about 30 children, and it is understandably very difficult to have the modes and procedures of years quite suddenly disrupted. It is disquieting to have other professionals enter their classrooms. But many regular teachers are discovering the advantages of consulting with specialists, using aides, and team teaching. In addition, regular classroom teachers are taking advantage of the "revolution" to expand their professional competencies by learning more about diagnosing educational needs of children; writing IEPs with special educators, school psychologists, and other specialists; and managing complex classroom operations. In many schools regular conferences on the progress of children with learning problems are giving classroom teachers new insights into their own attitudes and abilities. Many are challenged and encouraged to experiment with new procedures and methods. Teachers are also learning clinical methods of

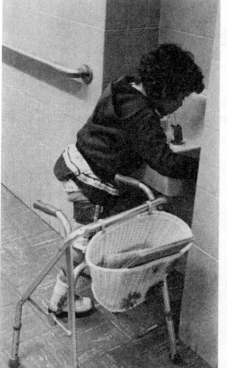

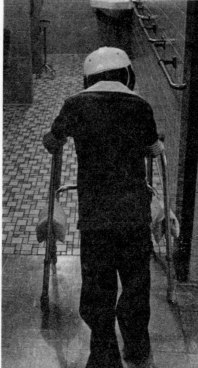

Top:
Student working
with hearing
impaired
classmates

Bottom left:
Helping herself

Bottom right:
Ramps and
hand bars are
aids to
self-help.

interviews in order to learn more from parents and to share with them their understanding of children's educational needs.

Teacher Preparation

Although the responsibility for carrying out the legal imperatives of P.L. 94-142 is placed directly on the public schools and their personnel, indirectly it extends also to the colleges and universities preparing personnel for schools. These institutions of higher education are, unfortunately, running about two years behind the public schools, but some changes are discernible. The Bureau of Education for the Handicapped (BEH) in the U.S. Office of Education has granted funds to more than 100 colleges in the form of Deans' Grants (Grosenick & Reynolds 1978) to stimulate the redesigning of teacher preparation in accord with the principles of P.L. 94-142; even more BEH funds have gone to state and local school systems for inservice teacher education. In addition, the states with few exceptions are using some funds provided under P.L. 94-142 to launch in the schools professional training programs of many kinds.

The needed personnel training ventures are beset with problems. Competent trainers are lacking in many subjects pertinent to the implementation of the Act. Time and resources within colleges of education limit the addition of important new training elements, and more inservice training programs add to the fatigue of already overburdened teachers. Also, teachers' unions and associations are imposing tough conditions and standards for training and program changes.

Early Education

The development of early education programs for handicapped children was a special concern expressed by the Congress in writing P.L. 94-142, requiring educational programs for children down to age 3 by 1978. In cases of contravening state law or practice, the mandate is inoperative. The Bureau of Education for the Handicapped grants to each state an extra $300 per handicapped child in the 3-5 age group who is served in a "free and appropriate" educational program, but a number of difficult problems are emerging.

In many cases there are not enough preschool programs for nonhandicapped children available in which to mainstream handicapped preschoolers. Also, controversies arise over the use of private schools for the public purposes of serving handicapped children and over the larger question of private vs. public development of preschool education. By and large, there has not been adequate attention given to recruitment and training of teachers to work with handicapped children at the preschool level. A more significant issue is the screening and classification system required for the young children, especially when the negative labeling of children is involved as a condition of receiving federal funds.

Change Process

The urgency of making the many-faceted changes in the schools cannot be overstated. Millions of handicapped children (estimated at 7-8 million in testimony before Congress) have been declared to have *present rights* to free, appropriate education. *Present* rights imply *immediate* service. Yet it is obvious that the changes involved, to run their full developmental course, are the work of a decade or more.

Because of the pervasive and difficult nature of the changes required, it is advisable to use systematic procedures for undertaking change and to include all levels of school personnel. If school board members and central office administrators (the superintendent and chief associates) do not acquaint themselves thoroughly with P.L. 94-142 and make early commitments to implementing its policies, how will school principals, teachers, and other school personnel take seriously the changes that are necessary?

Most critical of all, perhaps, is the early commitment and leadership of school principals and other middle-management personnel to vital implementation. Until they see a clear commitment by administrators and positive expectations for the new modes of education for handicapped students, teachers may resist both classroom changes and their indicated training. The change process will have full reality for regular teachers only when they see special education personnel assuming new roles and some of the supports coming into their classrooms.

Several systematic procedures for planning the change process are available, including approaches mainly oriented to *personal* aspects of change (Hall 1978), others that focus mainly on organizational changes and developments (Arends & Arends 1978), and still others that relate to training activities.

To Sum It Up

The changes that P.L. 94-142 is making in education for handicapped students portend changes in the philosophy, processes and structure of education for all students. If, by law, education must be individualized for handicapped students, then it is not inconceivable that the benefits of individualization will eventually be extended to all students. If free, public, appropriate education is provided for handicapped children in the 3-5 and 18-21 age range, then we must face the possibility that such education will be considered the right of all children. If program plans are negotiated with parents of handicapped children, should not this process be extended to the other parents as well? Many observers believe, based on the openers provided through P.L. 94-142, that major changes in the governance of the schools are in prospect.

In general, changes following from P.L. 94-142 focus on more inclusive arrangements within the public schools for students with a wide diversity of characteristics. As part of the total change, the efforts of special educators and regular teachers to forge a more integral working relationship should lead eventually to unification.

Currently, the new procedures for study and placement of handicapped children according to the provisions of the Act are running well ahead of changes in school structures and the training of school personnel for their new roles.

Educators need leadership in identifying the fundamental aspects of the new policies, organizing necessary training programs for school personnel, mounting efforts required in institutions of higher education, changing the attitudes of many educators and modifying the physical structure of schools. Like ideas, schools are tested at their margins; and today those margins are at providing equal educational opportunities for children who are handicapped, racially or culturally different, or are difficult to teach. Public Law 94-142 makes grand promises. Responding, delivering on these promises is an extraordinarily interesting and complex challenge to all schools.

References

Arends, R.I., and J.H. Arends. "Processes of Change in Educational Settings: An Application to Mainstreaming." J.K. Grosenick and J.C. Reynolds (Eds.), *Teacher Education: Renegotiating Roles for Mainstreaming.* Reston, Va.: Council for Exceptional Children, 1978.

Brown versus *Board of Education*, 347 U.S. 383 (1954).

Deno, E.N. (Ed.). *Instructional Alternatives for Exceptional Children.* Reston, Va.: Council for Exceptional Children, 1972.

Dimond, P.R. "The Constitutional Right to Education: The Quiet Revolution." *The Hastings Law Journal*, 1973, 24, 1087-1127.

Gilhool, T.K. "Changing Public Policies: Roots and Forces." M.C. Reynolds (Ed.), *Mainstreaming: Origins and Implications.* Reston, Va.: Council for Exceptional Children, 1976.

Grosenick, J.K., and M.C. Reynolds (Eds.). *Teacher Education: Renegotiating Roles for Mainstreaming.* Reston, Va.: Council for Exceptional Children, 1978.

Hall, G.E. "Facilitating Institutional Change Using the Individual as the Frame of Reference." J.K. Grosenick and M.C. Reynolds (Eds.), *Teacher Education: Renegotiating Roles for Mainstreaming.* Reston, Va.: Council for Exceptional Children, 1978.

Weintraub, F.J., A. Abeson, J. Ballard and M.L. Lavor (Eds.). *Public Policy and the Education of Exceptional Children.* Reston, Va.: Council for Exceptional Children, 1976.

Obstacles to Mainstreaming: How We Face Difference

STEVEN D. HARLOW
Center for Teaching and Learning
The University of North Dakota, Grand Forks

The major obstacles to provision of the best possible environment for the students with handicaps demonstrate a common tendency, the desire of the school to achieve instructional and social efficiency by removing and compartmentalizing difference rather than confronting it.

Recently I witnessed a school board meeting that seemed to pit the community (i.e., the school board) and school administration against the parents of an autistic child. The parents' brief essentially was that the district was responsible to provide the best available education for their child, while the board and the district were concerned with not establishing a precedent that would be quite costly.

To an educator this was depressing evidence that a great amount of attention focused upon the child with a handicap and the child with a school-related difficulty represents within the school legal rather than educational concerns.

While there will be need at times to invoke Public Law 94-142 on a reluctant school board, and even to establish "once and for all" that all children are entitled to full educational opportunity regardless of handicapping condition, we need to remind ourselves that formal hearings and board processes and discussions are bad educational examples. They emphasize the adversarial and the divisive.

The education of any child—but particularly a child with school-related difficulties—requires support, acceptance and cooperation. A legal decision on a handicapped child's right to the most enabling environment, though it implies educational treatment, must be thoughtfully and professionally translated from the judicial to the educational medium, and the responsibility for this translation should be the joint responsibility of the administration, the classroom teacher and the special education practitioner.

Perspectives

There are three ways of viewing the child with a problem or a handicap and dealing with difference within the school: the conservative, the approach piecemeal, and the humanistic.

Conservative View This view holds that the school represents a setting where each student is provided opportunity for an education, rather than a place where an education is guaranteed. If, for *whatever* reason, a child is unable to make use of the opportunity, that is not necessarily the school's obligation. Some more than others will be able to take advantage of their educational opportunity. The conservatives advocate minimizing special treatment for either the specially advantaged or the specially disadvantaged. Talent, motivation and achievement are the critical factors that will determine who will benefit most in the educative process. Some conservatives have modified their position to admit that certain students have physical or intellectual limitations to such a degree that they cannot benefit from the same opportunity given the nonhandicapped student. To such a conservative, the present arrangement of special education facilities is adequate. To experiment with different patterns of accommodations in dealing with the handicapped is a waste of resource. Strengthen existing facilities, the conservatives assert, but be wary of extending the definitions of handicapped, such as including those children with learning disabilities or severe behavioral problems. Those conservatives maintain a need for a separate, special education arm to deal with a narrowly defined group of children.

The fundamental conservative position advocates a laissez-faire setting where only the naturally advantaged child is encouraged, while the educative potentialities of other students are overlooked. Further, the position tends to neglect many forms of achievement that do not conform to the conventional mode. The modified conservative does not analyze the existing structure but takes for granted the value of the present arrangement of special education facilities. The modified conservative does not (perhaps cannot, because of his view of the handicapped) ask what occurs when children are categorized, then separated from their peers. Forgotten too is the question: what does it mean to educate a child who is designated handicapped?

The Approach Piecemeal Charles Frankel (1968) in discussing the approach to social problems piecemeal describes it as beginning "where the pain is actually felt" and defines its task as remedying the conditions that cause the pain. "Its function is remedial—to eliminate evils, not to realize an antecedent plan for good." This may be a definition of the approach to dealing with social problems that generated the special education arm of the school. Special education evolving bit by bit—piecemeal—became a response to the frustration, difficulties, pain that teachers in the regular classroom experienced in dealing with children with school-related problems. The special education arm removed both the "pain" and the responsibility of the regular teacher for educating such a child. As the special education arm began to grow, the "pain detectors" in the guise of psychodiagnosticians functioned to identify such potential pain carriers as the learning disabled, behaviorally disturbed, or educable mentally retarded before they could unfold as problems in the regular classroom.

Special education, the product of this fragmented approach, has focused upon disability and problem rather than upon the total child. The aim of education has been reduced to training if the child's handicap is an enduring one or correction if the problem is amenable to special efforts. One way or another, the task of the special education arm is to eliminate "pain" from the school.

"Efficiency" seems to be the key word. If we could reduce difference we could make the classroom environment accessible to more homogeneous approaches. A type of "slotsmanship" actually functions to select out those children who differ from the norm. The slots are special programs, each packaged with a label of disability or handicap. Defenders of this "efficiency" contend that the regular classroom has benefited, because the range of difference has narrowed to the point where teachers can dispense *more* instruction with predictable results. The child with school-related difficulties or a handicap is receiving a greater amount of attention through the special program.

The Humanistic View The third way of viewing the school and its response to the handicapped students starts with the premise that, as a humanistic institution, the school should be vitally concerned with both the development and realization of the students' best potentialities and the encouragement of cooperative group processes. Underlying both concerns is the *respect for human diversity*. Difference among students may be educative to all members of the school community. The school, and most properly the classroom, should be big enough to encompass many ways of learning, being and contributing. Shunting a child into an insular setting because of being intellectually slow or physically handicapped is an antagonistic function of the humanistic school.

We saw that the approach piecemeal attempts to ameliorate pain-producing conditions. If that fails, remove the pain (a student) from the mainstream. Humanistic orientation offers, first, a comprehensive picture of what the school and classroom should be. Instead of dividing the school into regular education for children who learn and adjust within the boundaries of conventional acceptance and special education for those who do not, the humanist asks the educational process to encompass difference and unity. From this perspective the objective of the school becomes one of linking the special education functions with the efforts of educating a *child*, not a special child.

From this third, humanistic perspective, we see that the task of the schools is to bring to the greatest degree possible the child with the handicapping condition or school-related difficulty into the mainstream, a monumental challenge. What is being envisaged is more than the handicapped child existing in an environment through the school day with

nonhandicapped peers. What is being proposed is two-fold: first, the creation of a learning environment that meets the academic needs of the child with difficulties; second, the creation of a social environment characterized by inclusion of all children. Both conditions are necessary in the education of every child. All children need the support of an environment where their strengths and difficulties are understood; they need mentors whose knowledge will facilitate their academic development. Children need to serve some social purpose in their environment and to make some contribution to the lives of other students.

The Stigmatization of the Handicapped

The term handicapped usually refers to an extant physical or intellectual condition limiting the person's ability to master certain situations, a permanent condition, to which the person has to accommodate himself. There are two important qualities in the definition.

First, the phrase "extant physical or intellectual condition" implies that the condition can be shown to exist by objective and verifiable means. When dealing with physical and sensory conditions objective verification does not pose a difficulty; similarly, when dealing with severe mental retardation, producing a reliable diagnosis presents no problem. But when determining mild retardation, emotional maladjustment or learning disabilities, valid and reliable measures are more difficult. Personal judgment of a professional is often the critical element in the identification of the handicap.

Second, the above definition emphasizes the *situational* nature of a handicap. The person is restricted in meeting the demands of certain situations but is *not* handicapped in others. The orthopedically handicapped student, for example, will face obvious restrictions in his ability to compete in athletic events, but his difficulties in mobility should have little effect upon his capacity to handle conceptual learning. Integral to the great advances in vocational rehabilitation are finding and creating *situations* where the person is not handicapped.

The important potential of the handicapped person facing nonrestricting areas is realized too infrequently. The specificity of the handicap is overlooked. What shows is the common tendency of both the handicapped person and others with whom he interacts to treat the handicap as a *total* condition pervading the entire life of the person, disqualifying that person from more effective participation in life. A reductive process occurs. *The person with a handicap becomes a handicapped person.* The total being is reduced to a handicap. A child is no longer an individual endowed with uniqueness, but instead becomes a member of a handicapped category.

There is, then, a wide difference between recognizing an extant handicap so that educational opportunities may be planned and stigmatizing a person as a handicapped individual. The first distinction recognizes an individual's limitations without losing sight of other qualities, while the second distinction rests solely upon the handicap. Recognizing the handicap in the school, while necessary, can lead to a point where a label becomes the currency of communication among school personnel. *It is not long before a label replaces the person.*

With this, an insidious phenomenon occurs: difference, which the label denotes, becomes equated with inferiority. As Goffman (1963) has written:

The attitudes we normals have toward a person with a stigma, and the action we take in regard to him are well known, since these responses are what benevolent social action is designed to soften and ameliorate. By definition, of course, we believe the person with a stigma is not quite human. On this assumption we exercise varieties of discrimination, through which we effectively, if unthinkingly, reduce his life chances.—By permission of Spectrum Books, Prentice-Hall, Inc., publishers, 1963.

Paradoxically, it is often through benevolence that we most critically reflect and reinforce the stigma. In providing a setting or modifying a schoolroom setting to accommodate the person with a handicap, we not only call attention to the handicap, but "pad" the school world. Too carefully delineating what a child can successfully handle may place that child in a fake world, a world the nonhandicapped child does not inhabit.

One characteristic of such a world is that success should be guaranteed to the handicapped child. Success is an important learning nutrient, but as a total diet it will lead to dependency upon the environment. From the nonhandicapped student we expect perseverance, even when achievement is not at all evident. The child with a handicap may have the environment modified to the extent that she or he has little practice with independent learning. Do the significant adults of the school really mean to say to the child, "We believe you are unable to handle frustration and make use of your mistakes."? If this is the unspoken prediction the adults in that school have predetermined, they have created a "reality" for the student with a handicap, a "reality" that is unfortunately out of step with the nonprogrammed real world.

The child with a handicap has more than an adversity to contend with. At first appearance, the handicap draws attention. Then second, the child's uniqueness is displaced by the label of the handicap. Third, he is treated in a way quite different from his nonhandicapped peer, has a specialist (e.g., a special education teacher, learning disabilities teacher) to teach him. In fact, there may be a special classroom for him and those like him. Both these situations may underscore and reinforce his difference. Fourth, educational regimen calls for a selection of tasks that the child can readily handle, cushioned in the educator's desire to have the child excluded from unpleasant or uncertain learning events. The consequence of the padded environment keeps the world of uncertainty and frustration at a distance. As a result, as time goes on the child will be less able to handle the uncertainty and frustration intrinsic to much of learning and functioning.

Fifth, the labeled child may be subtly convinced that he "cannot handle" much of what ordinarily would be explored and learned. The authoritative school attitude is that a child with a handicap can handle only so much and no more. This lessening of self-expectation becomes internalized. Instead of following the ostensible desire of the special education arm of the school that the child begin to feel he is able to achieve, the child instead feels less capable. After all, in the school situation he senses he is at a disadvantage with his nonhandicapped peers.

Still, that stigmatization is not entirely without benefit for the child with a handicap when he begins to realize that he is spared many of life's tasks that would normally be difficult and painful.

If all the besetting circumstances described above are permitted to become chronic and valid over all other situations, there will be a continuation of lower self-expectation, and the padded school environment that insulates the child from potential growth will render the child handicapped in a total way. The child is by attitude and orientation less and less able to handle the requirements of life. In a word, the child has become an invalid.

Bogus Handicaps

By the definition of handicapped offered earlier, many children now designated as learning disabled, emotionally disturbed, or even educable mentally retarded would not qualify as possessing a handicap. Many designated as learning disabled or behaviorally disturbed do not have a

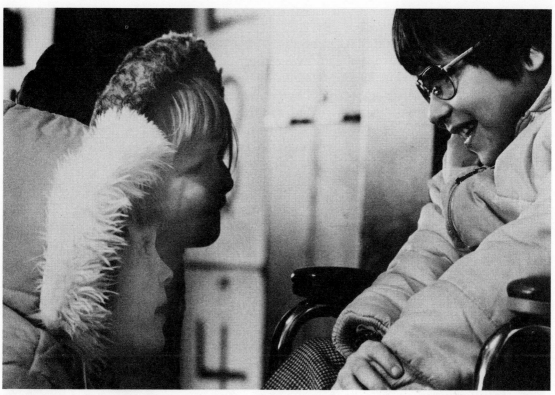

Classmates

With a little help from the special education teacher

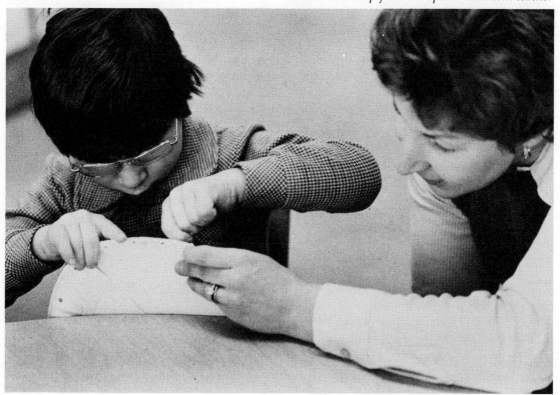

permanent condition that can be shown to exist by objective or verifiable means. Most children labeled as learning disabled or behaviorally disturbed are revealing school-related difficulties which, if properly understood and approached, need not be permanent. And although the school-related difficulties are changeable, unfortunately the handicapped label (e.g., learning disabled, emotionally disturbed) will hang on a long time. The label may, in fact, survive long after the child's school career is over.

The Honest Classroom

Mainstreaming is more than placing a child with a handicap in a regular classroom. Mainstreaming is best represented by the classroom with accommodations permitting the child with a handicap to function, to learn in an optimal fashion. Further, such a classroom provides a climate that encourages social inclusion with nonhandicapped peers, an honest climate where differences among persons are viewed as educative. Here non-handicapped children will encounter those they ordinarily would not. At first, such encounters may place the child with a handicap in startling contrast to the nonhandicapped peer, emphasizing differences. But as time passes, many children may acquire a broader view of life in which they observe how one human being makes adjustments and creates areas of meaning. Classmates will come to terms with the handicap, as does the child with the handicap himself. They will recognize which activities are precluded, which activities have to be modified and which are unaffected by the handicap.

Social inclusion, a characteristic of the honest classroom, closely resembles the "Melting Pot System for Children" described by Roger Barker (1978) as "the freedom to participate in behavior settings to the maximum of child's ability." Barker and his associates in their studies of many social situations found that assumption of responsibility by *all* children in the educational setting enhanced both the meaning of the individual to the group and the significance of the individual to himself. In talking about the child's participation in the Melting Pot System, Barker and Schoggen (1978) state:" . . .doing your part is especially valued, even if your part cannot be carried out with great effectiveness." The picture that emerges from this type of educational setting is one of vital inclusion, a place where each person without regard to level of ability or handicapping condition makes contributions and feels the significance of those efforts. This is not to say that all contributions are of equal value to the group, but it does indicate that the group would be diminished by the absence of any person's contribution.

Barker and Gump point out that the principal reason that the Melting Pot System produces this enhancement of each person is that it is based upon a "real need for student participation (Gump 1965)." Gump (1965) states that "It may also be significant that whether a person is marginal in the sense of being involved in the enterprises around him depends not only on his talent and background but also how much he is needed by these enterprises."

Responsibilities and duties in the social ambit of the classroom and the school may be designed in one of two ways: first, by reducing the number of roles students perform to only the most critical, a mode that after all happens to be the way of modern society; or, by disregarding efficiency and instead generating as many social tasks and options as are reasonably possible. We might aim to create duties and opportunities for individual expression in many situations. For example, a classroom that has a musical band could include every member of the class; or a classroom that has an art gallery could make a point of showing at least one product of each student. An even better example of inclusion might be the classroom with several small activities committees, each charged with planning and implementing a special product.

This kind of implementation of responsibility and duty values each student's potential contribution. In fact, if enough duties are generated everyone's contribution becomes essential to the functioning of that social microcosm. This mode will, in the end, prove to be the more productive environment for every student, with or without a handicapping condition.

Conclusion

In the near future, perhaps a smaller proportion of children with handicaps will be mainstreamed in the melting pot atmosphere than there should be. There may be many reasons to explain this, but it may be expressed by Maslow's maxim: ". . .if the only tool you have is a hammer, you treat everything like a nail." Having dealt piecemeal with school-related differences, we have developed its hammer—the special education arm of the school. The metaphoric hammer of the school also has a claw that functions to root out many persons representing difference.

The main impediment to social harmony is not diversity but intolerance. Efficiency of instruction as a goal of the school may well mask such intolerance. Professional educators, both regular and special, have a choice in proceeding with responsibilities. We may view our task as creating a climate truly devoted to the fulfillment of the child, a climate where uniqueness is dealt with in an open and honest manner, where difference is seen as educative and contributive rather than as deviant and inefficient, where education is conceived of as a process that creates as many life options as possible for all our children.

To realize this we must turn our attention to joint responsibilities and pull away from the divisiveness of the legal atmosphere that surrounds so many current decisions concerning children with handicaps. Special educator and regular educator must begin to collaborate in their mutual goal of finding instructional strategies that meet the academic needs of the child

The crippled child is not conscious of the handicap implied by his useless legs. They are often inconvenient or annoying but he is confident that they will never prevent him doing what he wants to do or being whatever he wishes to be. If he considers them a handicap it is because he has been told they are.

Having a normal mind my attitude to life was that of a normal child and my crippled limbs could not alter this attitude. It was when I was treated as someone different from the children with whom I played that my development had to include provisions to meet these influences that would have harnessed my mind to my crippled body.—From I Can Jump Puddles, "the best-known book ever written by an Australian." Alan Marshall, the author, suffered a crippling attack of poliomyelitis as a young child and went on to become one of Australia's most beloved and prolific writers. Reprinted with permission of the author.

with a handicap or school-related difficulties. To find such effective strategies may entail a great departure from the existing school structure of the two imperia: regular education and special education.

The borders should blur and with this, special and regular education may begin to talk, plan, and work together. As things stand now, frequently one hand does not know what the other is doing. A common element in this phenomenon is that the teacher (usually the special educator) with responsibility for the child possessing the school-related difficulty feels that he or she must have absolute answers or complete solutions to the child's school situation. Both regular and special teachers harbor the notion they should, in fact, be at such an omniscient level that they accordingly become defensive about communication with another professional for fear they will be "found out." To drop this folly and to realize that children are not puzzles to be solved by aid of diagnostic tests and kits is to begin the important process of communication among concerned professionals—professionals who do indeed possess expertness, but not the philosopher's stone.

Why attempt to compress the richness of diversity into two spheres, one for the "typical" and one for the "handicapped" or different? Perhaps we should remind ourselves as we work at our tasks that people, by their nature, are different.

References

Barker, R., and P. Schoggen. "Behavior-Generating Machines: Models Midwest and Yoredale." R. Barker, *Habitats, Environments, and Human Behavior*. San Francisco: Jossey-Bass, 1978.

Becker, E. *Revolution in Psychiatry*. New York: Free Press, 1964.

Frankel, C. "The Relation of Theory to Practice: Some Standard Views." H. Stein, *Social Theory and Social Invention*. Cleveland: Case Western Reserve Press, 1968.

Goffman, E. *Stigma*. New York: Spectrum Books, 1963.

Gump, P. *Big Schools—Small Schools*. Moravia, N.Y.: Chronical Guidance Publications, 1965.

Harlow, S. *Special Education: The Meeting of Difference*. Grand Forks: Rockefeller Fund North Dakota Study Group on Evaluation, 1975.

Harris, S. "Strictly Personal." *Grand Forks Herald*, January 11, 1979.

III. ". . .the most enabling environment"

Preparing Teachers for Special-Need Children in the Classroom

LILLIAN P. SHAPIRO
Bank Street College of Education
New York City

Enactment of mainstreaming legislation has aroused a good deal of controversy in educational circles, some of which stems from underlying political issues and professional attitudes toward general and special education that have not been brought clearly to the surface. Numerous presentations have appeared in print, in workshops and courses designed to assist educators in working with children in mainstreamed programs. These undercurrents must be addressed so that professional assistance offered teachers may be effective.

The causes, symptoms and intervention strategies for children with handicaps are complex, diverse and often unknown. No one professional discipline can be completely certain of statements made about a child's current or future functioning and potential, nor can one person acquire all the knowledge and skills required to diagnose and treat these children. The combined strength of shared observations and hunches from various clinical, therapeutic and educational disciplines, however, offers the hope of more precise and appropriate educational programming for children with special needs.

The confusion and conflict created by the implementation of PL 94-142 are similar in effect to every other sweeping legislative change that does not allow enough lead-in time for appropriate planning. Also some legislators who are more concerned with demonstrating to their constituency that they can provide "cost-effective" education have equated mainstreaming with inexpensive education. Thus, classes have been enlarged, supportive services have been reduced and some teaching jobs have been abolished. In addition, the wording of the law is still being interpreted. For example, the "least restrictive environment" is open to different meanings when decision-makers are faced with diversely handicapped children in communities having different types and qualities of programs available to them.

General and Special Education

For years most general educators have not had to deal directly with children with special needs. The problem of having to deal with conflicting feelings about what to do with them was effectively removed as the handicapped children were physically removed from the normal community and "cared for" in residential institutions. Disabled children remaining in the normal community were placed in segregated classrooms housed in separate buildings or in school basements. The legislative mandate has suddenly imposed on many teachers the responsibility of educating children whom they would not voluntarily have selected to teach. Unresolved feelings on the part of teachers not only interfere with their teaching practices but also affect developing attitudes of the nonhandicapped children toward their handicapped classmates. Equally destructive is the effect on the handicapped child's developing self-image.

In addition to uncertainties caused by political factors and their unresolved and often unrealized feelings about dealing with the handicapped, many teachers feel that ideologies and practices of special and general early childhood education are irreconcilable. Some special educators in their intense endeavors to improve the functioning of disabled young children often feel they must narrow the focus of their curricula on remedial, rehabilitative or therapeutic activities.

Early childhood educators are uncomfortable with the preponderance of structure, specificity and teacher mediation as practiced in special education classes, believing that such practices neglect young children's developmental needs and the "whole-child" approach that is an integral part of most early childhood curricula. Having long advocated the importance of free play, self-initiated activities and learning in the context of play situations, early childhood educators view special education practices as antithetical to these concepts. Education is made "special," however, by the attempt or ability of teachers to *modify usual teaching and learning processes to match the specialized needs of their children.* Instead of restricting a child's experiences, special techniques can be used to promote a child's growth and ability to learn from the environment. A special early childhood education program can be both developmentally based and humanistic in its approach and application, but it is most important that the usual early childhood curriculum be modified, taking into consideration the characteristics of young children with special needs who are different from those developing normally.

Curricula Modifications

Some characteristics of children with special needs include various degrees of inability to move independently, impaired sight and hearing, little or no overt curiosity in the environment, impaired memory, speech and language. A teacher needs some experience to distinguish between a

40

young child's intense involvement in an activity and perseverative behavior. The latter, characterized by repetitive and often frenzied behavior, requires specialized techniques to redirect the child into behavior less inhibiting to goal-directed performance and growth. Such problematic characteristics of special-need children demand greater teacher mediation than in ordinary classrooms and a conscious structuring and restructuring of materials, time and space. Children with special needs often have uneven developmental profiles that constantly challenge the teacher to create and present activities in which the children can use their strengths successfully so that they may be stimulated toward development in weaker areas. There are some special techniques and approaches usually found in special education programs that might help teachers develop enabling environments for children with special needs.

Although there are some positive implications in the early identification and intervention with young handicapped children, there can be certain negative side effects. When confronted with young children with specific labels who are admitted to programs designed to meet special needs, teachers often find they have certain expectations of such children. The label on the child and the phenomenon of the particular disability or handicap may accompany the child from one program to another. For this reason and because diagnostic labels are rarely helpful for individualized educational planning, teachers working with special-need children find that a problem-oriented approach is more effective than one that is category oriented. Implicit in a problem-oriented approach is the need for systematic observation of teaching and learning processes rather than primary interest or concern in the child's achievements. The *way* a child does a task or the *means* used can indicate what that child's problems and capabilities are.

Task Analysis

For a child with special needs, teachers will have to determine what skills are required for that child to succeed at his or her task. Awareness of these necessary skills not only fortifies the teacher with more information about the child's abilities or disabilities if he or she fails or succeeds at a given task, but also helps in future educational planning and goal setting. Tasks that will meet with more success can be presented to the child. Task analysis often requires fragmenting a child's learning experiences, an action particularly alien to early childhood programs. But this analysis used at appropriate times as a teaching tool can direct the child step by step to enjoy more typical early childhood experiences.

Many ordinary and daily abilities acquired relatively easily by normally developing children often take longer for the child with special needs and require more effort. Usually early childhood educators are confident that the provision of appropriate animate and inanimate environments is sufficient to promote learning in the normal child. They perceive active practice, drill and rote-learning activities as an intellectually destructive teaching mode. But for the special-need child, the educator's rationale for providing for practice of rather elementary and fragmented activities is that certain children with learning disabilities do not learn during the usual activities of the day as do children without learning handicaps. It is also important to equip those special-need children with as many automatic, useful behaviors as possible, such as numbers learned in counting games and songs, to release their energies for other learning experiences.

The Parent as Part of the Team

The parent who is, indeed, the young child's primary educator should be (and by law, is) considered an integral part of the evaluation and programming team. Although parents' observations and reports are not often considered to be the most objective sources of information about their children, parents' perceptions of their child can provide the important complementary information professionals lack because of their limited experiences with the child. All too frequently professionals prolong evaluation procedures or use ineffective educational and therapeutic techniques simply because they have neither the patience nor the foresight to ask or listen to parents' assessments of their child's problems.

Teacher and Child—Some Humanistic Considerations

A child's inability to communicate or some other disabling feature often elicits responding behavior from adults that turns into "treating the child as an object." Even young normal children with dependency needs and some older persons elicit this kind of dehumanizing behavior from their caretakers; they are treated as "objects." Talking about a child in his presence is one form of this treatment. Another example is that of the teacher who works intensively with a child on the development of certain cognitive skills, making that the sole purpose, while disregarding that child's social and emotional needs.

A special early childhood curriculum can be one that recognizes the developmental needs of young children across all physical and psychological dimensions of growth. Whether disabled or not, young children must have a variety of experiences within a stable, empathetic environment. All children need opportunities to find out about their environment and what they can and cannot do without the support of others. Specialized aspects of a curriculum can and should be incorporated in the context of developmentally appropriate experiences for young children.

So far, no procedures have been determined to be definitively correct or effective for all children with handicaps. Since there are, as yet, no foolproof programs, it is incumbent upon administrators and teachers themselves to apply a rationally based, flexible, eclectic approach to each child's individual problem. Whether such an approach is within the confines of a "program" or is simply experimental on a one-to-one basis, the result should be balanced experiences for each child's daily life.

The teacher who works with young children with special needs will continually be testing hypotheses about their developmental learning and behavior problems through systematic observation and task-analysis teaching techniques and making appropriate modifications in the curriculum. The teacher raises questions and shares observations about the children with colleagues in education and other collaborative disciplines, and especially with children's parents.

Just as there are no definitively correct procedures for all children with handicaps, so there is no perfect model for educational mainstreaming. Programs for introducing children with disabilities into the ordinary classroom need to be flexibly designed, adapted to the needs of both the normally developing child and the one with special needs and to the educational and general community's willingness and ability to provide appropriate services.

Children enjoy freedom of art expression.

The Pedagogy of Success

ASA G. HILLIARD III
Dean, School of Education
San Francisco State University, California

After decades of segregation, neglect, labeling and devaluation of children who are disabled and children who have been falsely identified as disabled or "handicapped," the tide seems to be turning. The "mainstream" movement is a remedy that received its impetus from legal challenges to professional practice and from legislative mandates. These court and legislative challenges are a reflection of the pressures on our system brought to bear by an increasingly conscious and assertive population who were supposed to be the beneficiaries of our special efforts to serve.

Educators as a group have not been in the forefront of the mainstreaming movement, but have rather tended to be in the first line of resistance. Even now, much of the mainstream effort represents our minimum attempt to accommodate ourselves to the mandates imposed upon us. The mainstream movement remains, among educators, more of a political than a pedagogical change. There is, as yet, little in the way of a reformulated philosophy and theory of education among professionals to guide our work to create a mainstream environment. In large measure, we continue to feel frustrated, overwhelmed, put upon, coerced because we hear from clients what they do not want, yet we do not have a clear sense of direction as to what they should want or what we should offer.

Faced with the problems created by an overnight return to the mainstream of all those children who have been gradually removed from the mainstream for isolated special treatment, we have accepted hastily fabricated educational practices, such as the concept of "individualized education" with its companion strategy, the "individual education plan (IEP)," and the generalized behavior modification orientation. Whatever the practical value these ideas and strategies may have for instruction, they seem to meet a more immediate need, which is that they are sufficiently different from general traditional practice in that they have a degree of "face validity" for clients.

They satisfy the need on our part to project the image that something special is being done for the "handicapped," that they are not left simply to languish. In part, this represents how deeply rooted our prejudices are toward human disability. If we saw children with disabilities as having unlimited potential despite the disabilities, we would have high expectations for them. We would make the same kinds of demands on them that we do of all other students, unless the disabilities clearly prevented their engaging in the common performance. The fact is that, given the way most classes are taught, few disabilities in themselves operate to *prevent* students from learning as well as students with no disabilities.

No one would deny that severe and profoundly disabled students require special attention and may well be limited in their ability to achieve in some school subjects. But we should keep in mind that those children are but a small fraction of those who have been identified as needing special education. By far the largest group of "disabled" children are classified as "learning disabled," "educationally handicapped," "emotionally handicapped," and "mentally retarded." Of the largest group, the "learning disabled," the largest subgroup is the "speech impaired." The largest subgroup among the "speech impaired" contains those children referred to a speech therapist for "articulation problems."

A disproportionately large number of cultural minorities and poor children who have no physical disability symptoms make up the population who are "disabled." For many of these children "articulation" problems are nothing more than culturally specific phonological patterns; "mental retardation" among many is nothing more than their failure to give the right answers to questions about European culture; "emotional handicap" is the label for their reaction to racism and other forms of aggression and hostility they have constantly experienced.

The return of these children to the mainstream will represent a threat to those of us who have rationalized them out of the mainstream in the first place. Moreover, the small proportion of children truly disabled, who may be described as "severely and profoundly handicapped," will be less of a threat to educators because of the problem that a disability itself creates for teaching than because of our deep fears of and consequent lack of comfort with persons who are hurt.

Strategies for Management and Control

The emerging pedagogy for students who are disabled emphasizes strategies for the *management* and *control* of student behavior. It also emphasizes a kind of "individualization" of strategies, which forces a student to learn alone, to follow a standard path at his or her own pace. This pedagogy, while not restricted in its application to children who are disabled, seems to meet our need to separate ourselves as teachers from personal encounters and *interaction* with children who are disabled. In a way, this pedagogy allows us to continue the isolation, segregation or quarantine of "special" children in a regular classroom.

Special children in a special classroom may also be kept at arm's length by this pedagogy. The mandates of Public Law 94-142 for "individualized" instruction and individualized learning or instructional *plans* tend to establish the teacher as a manipulator and the child as a respondent. The "evaluation" of mainstreaming is really more a matter of checking to determine whether teachers have followed the externally prescribed bureaucratic rules. Accountability has meant little more than that. Evaluation, diagnosis and decision-makers are, by law, placed in the context of adversarial proceedings. Somehow the child gets lost in all the adult rituals.

The mechanism and behaviorism dominating strategies for mainstreaming give rise to several problems:

(1) "Individualized" instruction *tends to ignore the individual,* since the "individual" plans grow out of the teacher's logic rather than out of the teacher-child interaction.

(2) Individual education plans, IEP, tend to allow children to vary their *pace but not their strategies and content for learning.*

(3) Prescriptions for professional practice do not grow out of a systematic study of known effective practice so much as out of armchair speculation.

(4) IEP or behavior modification approaches do not reflect an integrated educational theory and philosophy so much as a hurried *ad hoc* response to external pressures for "accountability."

(5) Much mainstream strategy focuses on plan-writing, record-keeping, negotiations rather than on close observation and analysis of children's responses.

(6) Much mainstreaming represents politics wearing the mask of pedagogy. Legislative and court mandates are written for punitive accountability.

Some Programs for Special-Need Children

It is my belief that regular pedagogy of high quality for the "disabled" children, those with special needs, can succeed. I believe also that this segment of the "disabled" population, constituting more than half the total "disabled" population, can succeed under regular or normal classroom pedagogy. To illustrate this, we must look to the data that come from the pedagogy of success, not from the autopsy of educational failure.

Let us examine in some detail the dynamics of four dramatically successful teaching programs said to be successful because they all involve direct work with learners identified as "disabled" by present professional standards. Such learners would include a large percentage labeled "mentally retarded," "emotionally handicapped" or "learning disabled," and among those are included large proportions of the poor, black, and "bilingual learners." Most would score, or actually have scored, very low on standardized IQ tests, and most would be regarded as school failures prior to entering the program of successful pedagogy. Many would be likely candidates for special education.

Four successful programs about to be described, while appearing to be quite different, have common elements embodied in "professional" theory and practice. These programs, their outstanding educator-creators and the teachers who implement them, present a stark challenge to those who perform other professional rituals to the letter but without evident success with the "disabled" students.

Three programs were designed for young children, one mainly for adults.

Ball-Stick-Bird Renee Fuller has shown that the relationship between intelligence test scores (IQ) and school achievement is a big fat zero, when all children get the same quality of instruction!:

Quite unexpectedly, severely retarded students, IQs in the 30s, learned to read with comprehension and perform academically with the system intended for superior students. By doing so, these low IQ students raised basic questions about the meaning of IQ tests and the concept of intelligence. These results should not have been obtainable if today's conceptualization of intelligence, abstract learning and IQ are correct. The initial results and their continued replication represent concrete data that something is wrong, not only with our IQ tests, not only with our concept of intelligence, but with our basic philosophy of education.—From *In Search of the IQ Correlation*, Ball-Stick-Bird Publications, Inc., Stony Brook, N.Y. By permission of author.

How does this happen? How does the Ball-Stick-Bird reading program work? Here are a few of the important features:

(1) Children are taught to read using a vocabulary they all know.

(2) "Level of difficulty" of vocabulary and alphabetical symbols is determined by research on the children who are served.

(3) "Complex" skills and concepts are learned early, before all the basic elements of the system are taught, thus dramatically improving motivation. For example, children can read a word after they have learned the first two letters and a sentence after learning the first four letters.

(4) Studies of how children treat content serve as the basis for design and revision of the program, rather than studies of children or their families.

(5) Content of the reading program is taken from space fiction, an area research has revealed to be of high interest among most children.

(6) The task of learning to read is not confused with other distracting tasks. For example, three simple shapes that can form all capital letters are selected, each shape with its own color to aid in identification. Lower case letters are learned after reading has been learned. Further, the alphabet sounds are not taught, since they have little use in reading. Rather, each letter is called by its usual phonetic sound.

48

unique assumption, that response is treated as a *new system*, which is respected by having others solve problems by that system.

(4) SEED teachers analyze their strategies by determining whether they are getting meaningful *questions* from students. They explore the reasons behind a technically correct answer. Is the student using the same assumptions as the questioner? Is the student answering the same question? Is the student answering at random? SEED teachers review logs to assess development of their strategies on development of students.

(5) SEED teachers use peer critique.

The individualization indicated above is clearly dependent upon the anticipated *actions* and *interactions* of the students, an individualization that the students cannot help but experience as directly responsive to them. Project SEED is social learning. Individualization is achieved, however, in a social, not an isolated, setting. The individual student's contribution is the real material of the classroom.

Paulo Friere Working with some of the poorest native Brazilian adults, Paulo Friere taught them to read in about thirty-six hours. How did Friere achieve this? He spent about twelve hours in discussion with his students (circle of culture). His aim was to get them to see and articulate the difference between natural (God-made) and cultural (man-made) things. By teaching this distinction in its broadest form, he helped students to become more conscious of themselves as culture makers. He made careful note of language students already used and recorded particularly vocabulary common to all, words containing three syllables and those with strong emotional value. As the "generative" word list, he used seventeen of these words containing all the phonetic sounds of Portuguese. When this list was learned in a certain way, in about twenty-four hours the student was a reader!

The Friere system, with its potential for application in classrooms with special-need children, reflects individualization in the reliance of the teacher on the experiences, vocabulary and culture of the student. Friere's emphasis is upon the *reciprocity* between teacher and student, a dialogue versus a monologue.

Oakland Community School This school, in a social setting, practices "individualization" with many children labeled "problems" or "difficult to teach," many among them preschoolers who are nearly classic cases from a social worker's notebook. Yet on standardized achievement tests, these children from Oakland's poverty pocket perform well above the nation's average in everything. How do they do it?

The individual child finds his or her identity as part of a group. Uniformity of action is not expected of these children. A classroom visit reveals an openness in all the children and an eagerness and freedom of participation that so many black children in America have had pressed out of them early in the school experience. "Individualization" is accomplished here; teachers have made the successful effort to know each child.

The Ball-Stick-Bird reading method is individualized in that it is d
to use *what children already know* in teaching them new things. Beca
responsive to their strong interests it is interactive, even though
appear to be prefabricated because of use of textbooks and st
content; it is interactive because content and standard material are
upon a high-quality estimate of knowledge and skills, intere
motivations, and patterns of learning possessed or used by the ch

Project SEED Designed by William Johntz, Project SEED is a pi
using mathematicians to teach college-level mathematical principl
problems to children from kindergarten through sixth grade.

On May 8 at the University of California, San Diego, I attended Mr. W.F.
demonstration of the technique he used to teach algebra to second and fift
students in his program of Special Elementary Education for the Disadva
"SEED." He simply taught a fifth grade class from Logan Elementary School
minutes. To say that I was impressed with the results is an understa
Children with obvious language problems responded correctly and enthusia
and asked very shrewd, insightful questions. . . . Mr. Johntz has undo
described to you his success in Berkeley where he says his mathematics p
has led children to greatly improve their performance in other subjects. M
information about these "side effects" comes from Mr. Johntz, but my
observation indicated clearly that the children do grasp concepts. . .and s
genuine intellectual curiosity which I would be glad to see more widespread
our graduate students at the University of California at San Diego.—Dr. G
Backus, Professor of Geophysics, University of California, San I
Hilliard 1976, p. 42.

Project SEED involves poor children, black children and brown chi
among others, who normally would be relegated to the mathematical
heap. It works! But how does it work? This way:

(1) Project SEED teachers start each class with a conceptual re
using the technique of periodical sequential review.
(2) Teachers keep a log for each child, which includes: samples c
dents' dialogue to illustrate the student's meanings, the teacher's tho
about the pupil; teacher's comments on successful techniques tried;
prehensive report of things covered.
(3) Interpersonal strategies are as follows: teachers have sp
techniques for making individual contact with each child; studer
trouble are never stigmatized; students are given a vehicle for intelle
protest; an atmosphere is created conducive to disagreement, eve
small numbers of children against the whole class; students are praise
catching the teacher's mistakes; the teacher gives the same kind of rea
to good questions as to good answers. When the student responds w

Common Themes

What do educational programs that *work* have in common? A great deal:

(1) In no case does "school success" require a change in the children, their families and their communities as a professional precondition for child growth.

(2) In every case the teaching approach is rooted in what Friere calls "dialogue," the systematic use of teacher-child interchange as the basic "material" for the design of ongoing classroom strategies. In the case of Friere and Johntz, the dialogue has an almost moment-to-moment impact on classroom action. In the case of Fuller and Huggins (Oakland Community School), the dialogue includes more pre-planned activities, which are, however, dictated by systematic uses of children's responses.

(3) In each case the strategies are built upon a systematic analysis of the reasons for student successes or failures.

(4) The individual's *responses* are the origin of instructional design ideas rather than analyses of what the learners did not do.

(5) Learning is a collaborative social process.

(6) Learning material comes from the cultural experiences of the group. If it does not already exist, a common experience is constructed.

(7) The highest premium is placed upon each student's creativity, using the emerging culturally specific materials as compared to the traditional reliance on standardized texts.

(8) "Advanced" intellectual ideas are taught from the beginning. Students do not have to wait to master everything teachers have thought were the basics or prerequisites. For example, learners have early encounters with abstract words, abstract mathematical ideas, and advanced political and/or philosophical concepts.

(9) The teachers possess both a deep knowledge of the subject matter as well as valid principles of learning.

(10) Instructional strategies are based on knowledge of how learning happens. Strategies are grounded in reality, and they are validated.

(11) There is a low failure rate.

(12) In no case is discipline a problem.

(13) Student motivation is very high, a major change.

(14) The teachers are working with the toughest problems but are getting the highest quality results.

(15) In no case are *standardized tests used for diagnosis in order to design instruction!*

(16) In no case are children tracked, even though many would "qualify" as cases for special education.

Conclusion

In almost all the many studies of teaching and learning, some of which are richly funded, "teaching" is treated as if it were a standard thing. Yet any sensitive observer knows that teaching quality varies. In each of the above programs we can see that the quality of teaching, almost alone, can make dramatic differences in instructional gains for learners. With such demonstrable evidence that there are ingenious, sane and humanitarian programs that do and will work for the educationally "disabled," we must place the responsibility for the development and application of valid pedagogy right where it belongs, with us teachers.

Children may have disabilities, and many have "special needs," but the special need all children have is the kind of teachers who can and will make such programs effective.

Mainstreaming will be a success when we stop labeling children with handicaps—whatever that limitation may be, physical, behavioral, cultural or racial. But that is not enough. We must offer *skilled teaching* to all children.

Selected Bibliography

Coleman, M. *Black Children Just Keep on Growing: Alternative Curriculum Models for Young Black Children.* Washington, D.C.: National Black Child Development Institute, 1977.

Fuller, Renee. *In Search of the IQ Correlation: A Scientific Whodunit.* Stony Brook, N.Y.: Ball-Stick-Bird, P.O. Box 592, 1977.

Granger, R.C., and James C. Young. *Demythologizing the Inner-City Child.* Washington, D.C.: National Association for the Education of Young Children, 1976.

Hilliard, Asa G., III. "The Strengths and Weaknesses of Cognitive Tests for Young Children." In J.D. Andrews (Ed.), *One Child Indivisible.* Washington, D.C.: National Association for the Education of Young Children, 1975.

———— *Alternatives to IQ Testing: An Approach to the Identification of Gifted "Minority" Children,* final report to California State Department of Education, 1976 Special Education Support Unit, ERIC Clearinghouse on Early Childhood Education, ED 147009.

Hilliard, Asa G., III, and K. Windsor. *I'm Back! Children's Social Behavior: Assessment Criteria* (Head Start Profiles of Program Effects on Children). Westport, Conn.: Mediax, Inc., 1978.

Houts, Paul (Ed.) *The Myth of Measurability.* New York: Hart, 1977.

Illich, Ivan. *Medical Nemesis.* New York: Bantam, 1976.

Pearce, Joseph Chilton. *Magical Child.* New York: E.P. Dutton, 1978.

Rist, Ray C. *The Urban School: A Factory for Failure.* Cambridge, Mass.: Massachusetts Institute of Technology, 1973.

Schrag, P., and D. Divoky. *The Myth of the Hyperactive Child and Other Means of Child Control.* New York: Pantheon, 1975.

Releasing the Child's Potential: Parent-Community Resources

BETTY H. WATERS
Department of Education
North Georgia College, Dahlonega

The goal of mainstreaming must be that of reaching the needs of each child and not of serving a cause. The classroom teacher and the specialist, upon whom the burden falls of implementing the mandate, should have every available resource to work toward a well-planned individualized program for each student.

In order to plan adequately for this enormous challenge, teachers will need to know everything possible about each child with a handicap or learning problem before that child enters the classroom. Not all this will be feasible, of course, before entry. Much will be learned only after the child has come into the mainstream of the classroom and has been under observation, study and perhaps testing over a period of time.

The information vital to knowing and understanding the child with special needs will be as comprehensive as can be obtained, such as:

1. Physical developmental patterns/accomplishments
2. Learning processes:
   a. Visual: association, memory, figure ground
   b. Auditory: association, memory
   c. Language: receptive, expressive
   d. Nonverbal functions: temporal orientation, laterality, directionality
3. Academic skills: reading, spelling, grammar, math, science
4. Fine motor skills: handwriting, art
5. Social skills: with peers, with adults, in groups, on one-to-one basis
6. Specific handicaps due to illness, injury
7. Modifications needed because of handicap or illness (i.e., ramps for wheelchair or medications to be taken during school hours)
8. Specific family problems that might affect the adjustment of the student

Developmental tests given by the classroom teacher can be most successful in securing much of the needed information as outlined above. Two excellent developmental inventories are: Gainer, William L., Richard L. Zweig, Phyllis W. Dole, Sandra A. Watt, (Eds.) *Santa Clara Inventory of Developmental Tasks,* Richard L. Sweig Associates, Inc., Santa Clara, California, 1974; and Mann, Philip H., and Patricia Suiter, *Handbook in*

Mothers and teachers working with hearing-impaired children

Diagnostic Teaching: A Learning Disabilities Approach, Allyn and Bacon, Inc., 1974.

The regular classroom teacher and the special teacher should each work on completing the inventory and compare findings. Further than this, questionnaires can be developed to be completed by the parents so that information on the developmental patterns and chronological ages of acquisition can be added to the case history of each student.

Working with Parents

The teacher working with parents of children with special needs must be aware of the fears and anxieties that are usually of dynamic concern within the child's family. Leo Buscaglia lists these concerns held by most parents: "What is going to happen to this child?" "If he is different, will I be able to educate him?" "What are my friends going to say?" "What did I do?" "Did we get the right doctors?"

The initial conference with the parents is most important. The professional team of classroom and special education teachers will want to hold that conference in an atmosphere of accepting warmth toward child and parents, realizing most certainly that these parents hold great love for their children. The parents' abilities to understand and help their children will depend on their own acceptance of the child as well as how others in the family and those in their community have accepted their child and themselves. At the first conference, a "listening and understanding" session, professional findings should be reported to the parents and some specific instances given as to ways parents can help their child both at home and in support for the preparation for school. After a mutual trust has been established (and this is imperative), parents can then be involved in specific, meaningful tasks:

1. Keeping of anecdotal records of home successes and problems
2. Maintaining consistent behavior tasks decided by teaching team
3. Providing language development opportunities: reading aloud, retelling stories, cutting and pasting pictures from magazines to develop classification skills (for example, all the electric machines, all the farm animals, yellow things)
4. Providing physical exercise for gross and fine motor activities
5. Providing enrichment trips
6. Parent involvement as members of a school-wide advisory board, or as an advisory board for one specific classroom
7. Publishing by parents of newsletter of classroom happenings
8. Volunteering as aides
   Parents make excellent aides, as they are usually aware of needs of all children and are likely to be appreciative of the extra efforts on behalf of children that school professionals make each day.
9. Making curriculum materials
   Parents working closely with teachers can offer many skills in providing and making vital curricula materials or can volunteer to get funds for purchasing needed materials.
10. Giving support to inter-team community exchange
    Parents working together to help the school and their children, by developing excellent rapport/understanding among themselves, are better able to cope with common problems. One such parent remarked: "It means a lot to know that some of our problems with our child are not because of *us* but because of his unique perceptions. Having other parents to share with us has made a world of difference."
11. Working with community commissioners, state legislators, national organizations
    Parents can disseminate awareness of educational needs to those making important decisions regarding budgets for education.

Conducting inservice training for parents depends on numbers of parents, professional staff available, space and time factors. The training, which is vital for the effectiveness of parents as helpers, should be started before parents begin to work either in the classroom or as help from the home, and there should be continual training as long as feasible.

When talking with parents and working with their children, the professional staff member must always be conscious of the responsibility of returning dignity to the parents and child. Rehabilitation is far more possible when there is improved self-concept.

Peers Can Help

When arranging for other children in the classroom to work as peer-tutors and to assist students needing help, the classroom teacher can prepare materials in advance such as skill sheets or other adjuncts to teaching and learning. It is absolutely necessary that the peer-tutor be a courteous assistant. A peer-tutor with a negative approach may create a rejection atmosphere, which can be disastrous not only to the child with special needs who should be helped, but for the entire classroom. It is often an excellent motivating force for an older student from another classroom, who is reading below grade level, to tutor in the primary grades. This older student may gain confidence in his or her ability to read while enabling that younger student to progress, thus creating a two-fold benefit.

Peer tutors can assist: in learning centers, in reading to younger students, in learning sight words, in learning spelling words, with fine motor exercises, with gross motor exercises, in math drill exercises, in answering questions regarding skill work, or with crafts.

It is inadvisable, because of their inexperience, to have peer-tutors introduce new materials or skills, nor should they make any attempt to assist in counseling with students.

Community-Organizational Resources

The principal and other professional staff can assist parents and classroom teachers in acquiring materials as well as special services for special-need students from the various resources in the community or beyond from such organizations as:

American Association for Health, Physical Education, and Recreation (AAHPER), 1201 16th Street, N.W., Washington, D.C. 20036, has a unit devoted to research in better programs of recreation and physical education for the handicapped, with findings published as papers and pamphlets. Health and safety problems of the handicapped are concerns of AAHPER.

American Association of Workers for the Blind, Inc. (AAWB), 1151 K Street, N.W., Suite 637, Washington, D.C. 20005, disseminates information on preventing blindness. Promotion of work possibilities for the blind is included in their goals. Write for information on obtaining their published materials.

The American Legion, National Child Welfare Division, P.O. Box 1055, Indianapolis, Indiana 46206, emphasizes services to children of veterans. Contact local American Legion for further information.

Civitan International, 1401 52 Street South, P.O. Box 2102, Birmingham, Alabama 35201. Civitan International Clubs all over the United States seek ways to help the handicapped. Contact your local club for more information.

Joseph P. Kennedy, Jr. Foundation, 719 13th Street N.W., Suite 510, Washington, D.C. 20005, supports research for the prevention of mental retardation. They sponsor Special Olympics, Inc., which offers nationwide experiences for retarded students. Write for brochures and pamphlets.

Muscular Dystrophy Association of America, Inc., 1790 Broadway, New York City 10019, sponsors research into causes of muscular dystrophy, distributes their materials nationwide. Write for further details.

References

Ames, Louise Bates, Clyde Gillespie, and John Streff. *Stop School Failure.* New York: Harper and Row, 1972.

Braun, Samuel J., and Miriam G. Losher. *Are You Ready To Mainstream?* Columbus, Ohio: Charles E. Merrill, 1978.

Burton, Lindy. *The Family Life of Sick Children: A Study of Families Coping with Chronic Childhood Disease.* London: Routledge & Keyan Paul, 1975.

Buscaglia, Leo F. "Parents Need To Know: Parents and Teachers Work Together," Samuel A. Kirk and Jeanne McRae McCarthy, (Eds.), *Learning Disabilities,* Selected ACLD Papers, 365-377. Boston: Houghton Mifflin, 1975.

Dennis, Wayne, and Margaret W. Dennis. *The Intellectually Gifted: An Overview.* London: Green and Stratton, 1976.

Dreikurs, Rudolf. *Coping with Children's Misbehavior: A Parent's Guide.* New York: Hawthorn Books, Inc., 1972.

Dunn, Lloyd M., (Ed.), *Exceptional Children in the Schools: Special Education in Transition.* New York: Holt, Rinehart and Winston, 1973.

Gerheart, B.R. *Learning Disabilities, Educational Strategies.* New York: Peter H. Wyden, Inc., 1970.

Gowan, John Curtis, George M. Demos, and Charles J. Kokaska, (Eds.). *The Guidelines of Exceptional Children.* New York: David McKay, 1972.

Grosse, Susan J., and Monica C. Becherer. *Physical Education Activities for the Uncoordinated Student.* West Nyack, N.Y.: Parker Publishing Co., Inc., 1975.

Hall, Joanne E., and Barbara E. Weaver, (Eds.). *Nursing of Families in Crisis.* Philadelphia: Lippincott, 1974.

James, Reginald L., and Donald L. MacMillan, (Eds.). *Special Education in Transition.* Boston: Allyn and Bacon, Inc., 1974.

Kirk, Samuel A. *Educating Exceptional Children.* Boston: Houghton Mifflin, 1972.
———, and Jeanne McRae McCarthy, (Eds.). *Learning Disabilities,* Selected ACLD Papers. Boston: Houghton Mifflin, 1975.

Nesbitt, John A., Paul D. Brown, James F. Murphy, (Eds.). *Recreation and Leisure Service for the Disadvantaged.* Philadelphia: Lea and Febiger, 1970.

Patterson, Gerald R., and M. Elizabeth Gullian. *Living with Children, New Methods for Parents and Teachers.* Champaign, Ill.: Research Press, 1973.

Salk, Lee. *What Every Child Would Like His Parents To Know.* New York: David McKay, 1972.

Sianty, Mary Lou de Leon, (Ed.). *The Nurse and the Developmentally Disabled Adolescent.* Baltimore: University Park Press, 1977.

Spock, Benjamin. *Problems of Parents.* Boston: Houghton Mifflin, 1962.

Strang, Ruth. *Helping Your Gifted Child.* New York: E.P. Dutton, 1960.

The Year We Had Aaron

MOLLY OAKLEY

Teacher, Second Grade
Cambridge Central School, Cambridge, New York

As a teacher, my reaction to "mainstreaming" is one of pure panic. My pulse quickens when I hear the word and I am reminded that mandatory mainstreaming is going to mean new problems for my class and me, problems I can anticipate but cannot even identify. How can I possibly care for and teach those children who need special and individual treatment? How can I presume to teach as well as those with specialized training and diagnostic skills?

When my panic subsides I remind myself mainstreaming is not new to my classroom. I have had an experience that has taught me a lot about "fear" and "difference" and "effects on other children." I realize now that perhaps the experience was not as excruciating or even as threatening as I had feared, but it was frightening, the worry of it was constant, and it was grimly positive. It was a totally human and special experience, and no one in my second grade class that year will ever be the same because of it.

Aaron entered my class on the first day of school in September. Though he was new in our district, I already knew quite a lot about him. From his folder and notes from his parents I had learned that Aaron had bone cancer, that he was undergoing radiation treatment, and that his prognosis was poor. It was feared that he would live only another six to ten months.

I recognized Aaron the minute he walked in. His eyes which were alert and wide looked even bigger because he had no hair. But his smile was friendly, if a little rebellious. His physique was strong though lean for a second-grader.

When I saw that the children were afraid of him I realized that helping Aaron included helping the children understand and accept him. Shortly after the term began, during one of Aaron's absences that were to become more frequent, we had our first discussion. I told the class we had to talk about somebody important to all of us, Aaron. "Why is he bald?" was the first question. "Why is he absent so much?" "Why doesn't he have to take gym?" "Why can't he play with us out on the playground?" Their questions showed that there was already a feeling that Aaron was different.

I explained that he had an illness that tired him easily, that the medicine he took was making his hair fall out. I continued: "How would you like starting a new school feeling strange, with no hair, knowing you looked peculiar?" "How would you feel trying to make new friends and feeling tired and ill at the same time?" I didn't go lightly with them. I was hard on them, not chastizing but really letting them feel for fifteen minutes Aaron's skin and tears and loneliness.

Right away, the next day in fact, the classroom was more relaxed and the children at once began to defend Aaron to the other children in the school lunch line, at the bus stop, and on the playground. They were not going to tolerate others' acting as they had been acting, afraid of a difference.

The first few months Aaron did well in school. He enjoyed reading and searched the library shelves for dinosaur books. He loved looking after our new cage of mice, and for Christmas he made the class a huge "pin-the-tail-on-the-mouse" game. He was alert and seemed strong with a strength that could easily be translated into stubbornness, even an arrogance that shrieked independence.

Shortly after Christmas Aaron started getting weaker and had to cut down school to half a day, alternating mornings and afternoons. More frequently now I had to talk to the class. I gathered them all on the rug in our small library section. Huddled close together, we talked about how to help Aaron more. I reminded them how hard it must be to be ill for so long.

After a time he was almost never able to come to school. At one of our library corner discussions we decided to buy Aaron a gerbil cage to house two mice from our rapidly growing family. We selected four children from the class to accompany me in a visit to Aaron with the cage, two mice, and a fifty-pound bag of wood shavings. He was delighted with his gift. The visit was such a success that we began going weekly. Each Thursday four children, a different quartet each time, crowded into my dilapidated VW with presents, letters and more wood shavings for the mouse cage. Though Aaron was not in class each day, he was still one of us. We would not let his absence exclude him from our activities.

Aaron came back to class once more. That day he was suffering, and he could not help complaining about pain in his back. His parents and I had decided he should try to endure this two-hour rescheduling. We tried to make him as comfortable as possible with sleeping mats piled for support on his chair. He sat through math and an art project, and he must have been in agony, for only two days later we learned that the cancer had spread to his back and that his spinal cord had disintegrated in that area, the cause of his severe pain that day.

The announcement a day or two later that Aaron was in the hospital was accepted by the class in sober silence. Huddled again in our library ring, we talked in a new way about Aaron's illness. Till that time I had never mentioned cancer, for as long as Aaron himself was unaware of the nature of his illness, I felt it would be unfair to divulge this to the class. But after conferring with his parents, I told the children that Aaron had cancer.

The ability of these second-graders to understand astounded me. I should have known that cancer was no stranger to some who had had relatives who died of it or were suffering from it now; I should have remembered they learned more from television than we adults liked to admit.

But I did not get the full impact of their maturity until Margaret asked: "What are his chances?" My answer, "Not good." Margaret persisted. "I don't mean that. What are the percentages that he'll not live?" In my surprise I blurted out, "Ninety to ninety-five." Margaret got her answer, and she burst into tears.

The class was stunned by this new dimension to our problem, for now they did not perceive this as Aaron's problem or even his parents' problem but a part of their own family hurting and suffering. When Aaron's mother called me a week later I was overjoyed for I had not expected to see Aaron again. Not only was Aaron better, he was home from the hospital. Would I like to talk to him? What a wonderful moment, to hear his happy voice on the telephone!

Aaron did not come to school again. We made one more visit, then no more because the excitement of seeing his classmates tired him. May and June were long months. The joy of spring and the marvel at what had been accomplished as a class that year were contrasted with our concern and worry for one of us. We continued sending a stream of letters, drawings, little books and puzzles. Whenever one of us felt the need, we had one of our intimate library talks. The children tried to understand how the suffering felt and why it could not be stopped. As a teacher, I was trying to prepare them for Aaron's death. While we talked about hope and strength, we did discuss death, and it was understood that Aaron might die soon.

While my principal knew and approved of the direction I had taken in preparing the children for the probability of Aaron's death, several teachers were disapproving. I should not be making such a big deal, they said. But I could not imagine ever ignoring my second-graders' thirst for answers and understanding. I could never insult their keenness and openness by playing with their love of a friend or their fear for him. They had to discover and fulfill their need to grieve.

On the last day of school, June 22, 1977, we gathered on the library rug. I told the children that Aaron had died that morning. We cried together. Then I answered questions. It was important to the children that he had died at home and not at the hospital. Despite their sophistication in knowing about cancer, they were young children after all. They asked many questions about how Aaron felt when he died, how his parents felt. Did Aaron have his teddy bear with him? Did it go with him? Was he in pain now?

In our class book we wrote the last entry, "Aaron died today. We loved him very much," and we pasted in a picture of him taken at our fun-filled silly Halloween party so long ago.

The bell rang. I handed out the report cards. Then the children left, and I left, scattering to the summer, never to come together again to huddle in the library corner. We took our grief for Aaron with us.

The above is printed with the permission of David and Pamela Jackson, parents of Aaron, who say: "We were very fortunate that Molly Oakley dealt with the problems she describes in her article with deep understanding and love to her professional responsibilities, to Aaron, and to her students."

Some Teaching Resources

BEVERLY BREKKE
JERRY WELLIK
HARRY WEISENBERGER
Center for Teaching and Learning
The University of North Dakota, Grand Forks

These teaching resources are for you, the classroom teacher concerned with the mainstreaming of handicapped children. While these children may have some special needs, they also have needs that are common to all children. Children differentiated on the basis of their handicaps frequently become limited by a functional impairment imposed upon them by others. These resources may suggest ways for you to create a personalized approach to an enabling environment, a place where children may be valued as whole persons, not part persons because of a handicap.

Periodicals and Articles

Birch, J.W. *Mainstreaming: Educable Mentally Retarded Children in Regular Classes.* Reston, Va.: Council for Exceptional Children, 1974. (ERIC Document Reproduction Service No. ED 090 724).

Brekke, B., S.D. Harlow, M.L. Lindquist, and M. Olson "Mainstreaming Special Education." *Insights,* 1976, 8 (Whole No. 5).

Cohen, S. "Integrating Children with Handicaps into Early Childhood Education tion Programs." *Children Today,* 1975, 4 (1), 15-17.

Dequin, H.D. "Selecting Materials for the Handicapped. A Guide to Sources." *Top of the News,* 1978, 35 (1), 57-66.

Guralnick, M.J. "Value of Integrating Handicapped and Nonhandicapped Preschool Children." *American Journal of Orthopsychiatry,* 1976, 46, 236-245.

Leckie, D.J. "Creating a Receptive Climate in the Mainstream Program." *Volta Review,* 1973, 75 (1), 23-27.

Levitt, Edith, and Shirley Cohen. "Attitudes of Children Toward Their Handicapped Peers." *Childhood Education,* 52, 3 (Jan. 1976):17173.

Lewis, E.G. "The Case for 'Special' Children." *Young Children,* 1973, 28 (6), 368-374.

Martin, E.W. "Some Thoughts on Mainstreaming." *Exceptional Children,* 1974, 41 (3), 150-153.

Rausher, Shirley R. "Mainstreaming: A Return to Yesteryear?" *Childhood Education,* 53, 2 (Nov./Dec. 1976): 89-93.

Zufall, D.L. "Exceptional Person: Approaches to Integration." *Journal of School Health,* 1976, 46, 142-144.

Bibliographies

Fein, R.L., and A.H. Ginsberg. "Realistic Literature About the Handicapped." *Reading Teacher,* 1978, *31* (7), 802-805.

Glockner, M. *Integrating Handicapped Children into Regular Classrooms.* Urbana, Ill.: University of Illinois, 1973. (ERIC Document Reproduction Service No. ED 081 500)

Klein, J. *Teaching the Special Child in Regular Classroms.* Urbana, Ill.: University of Illinois, 1977. (ERIC Document Reproduction Service No. ED 136 902)

Volkmore, C., and A. Langstaff. *Bibliography on Mainstreaming.* Los Angeles: California Regional Resource Center, 1975.

Books

Cleary, M. *Please Know Me As I Am.* Sudbury, Mass.: Jerry Cleary Co., 1975.

Gearhart, B., and M. Weisham. *The Handicapped Child in the Regular Classroom.* St. Louis: C.V. Mosby, 1976.

Glover, J., and A. Gary. *Mainstreaming Exceptional Children: How To Make It Work.* Pacific Grove, Cal.: The Boxwood Press, 1976.

Harlow, S. *Special Education: The Meeting of Differences.* Grand Forks, N.D.: University of North Dakota Press, 1975.

Jordan, J.B. (Ed.). *Teacher, Please Don't Close the Door—The Exceptional Child in the Mainstream.* Reston, Va.: Council for Exceptional Children, 1976.

Lowenbraun, S., and J. Affleck. *Teaching Mildly Handicapped Children in Regular Classes.* Columbus, Ohio: Charles E. Merrill, 1976.

Metsker, C., and E. King. *Hints and Activities for Mainstreaming.* Dansville, N.Y.: Instructor Publications, Inc., 1977.

Films

A Child Is a Child. (Film) AIMS. 1973. 16mm. Sound. 7 minutes. Color.

An Integrated Nursery. (Film) Bureau of Education for the Handicapped. 1973. 16mm. Sound. 15 minutes. Color.

Cipher in the Snow. (Film) Brigham Young University. 1973. 16mm. Sound. 24 minutes. Color.

School Is for Children. (Film) AIMS. 1973. 16mm. Sound. 17 minutes. Color.

The Madison School Plan. (Film) AIMS. 1972. 16mm. Sound. 18 minutes. Color.

Organizational Resources:

Alexander Graham Bell Association
  for the Deaf
3417 Volta Place, NW
Washington, DC 20007 (202) 337-5220

American Foundation for the Blind, Inc.
15 West 16th Street
New York, NY 10011 (212) 924-0420

American Speech and Hearing
  Association (ASHA)
9030 Old Georgetown Road
Washington, DC 20014 (301) 530-3400

Association for Children with Learning
  Disabilities (ACLD)
5225 Grace Street
Pittsburgh, PA 15236 (412) 881-1191

Council for Exceptional Children (CEC)
1920 Association Drive
Reston, VA 22091 (703) 620-3660

National Association for Retarded
  Citizens (NARC)
2709 Avenue E, East
Arlington, TX 76011 (817) 261-4961

National Center on Educational Media and
  Materials for the Handicapped (NCEMMH)
The Ohio State University
Columbus, OH 43210 (614) 422-7596

National Easter Seal Society for Crippled
  Children and Adults, Inc.
2023 West Ogden Avenue
Chicago, IL 60612 (312) 243-8400

"WE SPEAK for all the children of all the nations, all the lands, knowing well that in their common human core is more of likeness than of difference, knowing too that only as we reach that common core in children will men the world over reach it in each other." So spoke Agnes Snyder, an early leader, of the purpose of the Association for Childhood Education International.

Founded in 1892 as the International Kindergarten Union, the organization became the Association for Childhood Education in 1930. The National Council of Primary Education merged with the Association the next year. "International" was added to the name in 1946. Membership is open to all concerned with the education and well-being of children. Teachers, parents, college students, teacher educators, pediatricians, day care and community workers and others help make up the membership in 70 countries, mostly in active branches but also through individual memberships.

ACEI works to promote desirable conditions, programs and practices for children from infancy through early adolescence. Members strive to inform the public of the needs of children and work for the education and well-being of all children. ACEI's active publishing program includes an award-winning journal CHILDHOOD EDUCATION, bulletins, pamphlets and position papers. For further information about ACEI programs and membership or for a free publications catalog or copy of the journal, write to:

ASSOCIATION FOR CHILDHOOD EDUCATION INTERNATIONAL

3615 Wisconsin Avenue, N.W., Washington, D.C. 20016